MISSIONS BEYOND THE DIASPORA:

LOCAL CROSS-CULTURAL MINISTRY OF CHINESE CONGREGATIONS IN THE SAN FRANCISCO BAY AREA

Enoch Wan & Mike Hung Lei

MISSIONS BEYOND THE DIASPORA: LOCAL CROSSCULTURAL MINISTRY OF CHINESE
CONGREGATIONS IN THE SAN FRANCISCO BAY AREA

Copyright © Western Seminary: Center for Diaspora and Relational Research

DIASPORA
Series

Book **5**

**WESTERN
SEMINARY**
Center for Diaspora
and Relational Research

ISBN : 978-1-949201-05-5
December   2019 First Printing
Copyright : 2019 by Western Seminary Press
Center for Diaspora & Relational Research
Western Seminary
5511 SE Hawthorne Blvd.
Portland, OR 97215, USA

TABLE OF CONTENTS

ii

CHAPTER 1
INTRODUCTION

The background of the book

The two authors worked together for several years in the long process of designing the research toward the completion of this volume. It began with the doctoral studies of Mike Lei under the directorship of Enoch Wan at Western Seminary, leading to the completion of the dissertation by Mike Lei, "Missions Beyond the Diaspora: Local Cross-cultural Ministry of Chinese Congregations in the San Francisco Bay Area," (2017). Case study research and implementation of the research design, on the two local congregations was a post-doctoral study for the completion of this book.

The purpose of the book

This book is written with the purposes listed as follows:

A. To conduct archival research on the history of Chinese diaspora in the SFBA, the history and development of Chinese diaspora churches in the SFBA, local cross-cultural ministries of Chinese diaspora churches in the SFBA;

B. To contextualize diaspora missions and cross-cultural ministry training for Chinese diaspora in the SFBA;

C. To present ethnographic description of local cross-cultural ministries of two selected Chinese diaspora churches in the SFBA;

D. To derive missiological implications for local cross-cultural ministries of Chinese diaspora churches in the SFBA.

The organization of the book

Together with the Introduction (Chapter 1) and Conclusion (Chapter 7) in this book, there are seven chapters: historical study (Chapter 2), diaspora missiology (Chapter 3), local cross-cultural ministry of Chinese congregations in the San Francisco Bay Area (Chapter 4), contextualized training (Chapter 5), and case studies (Chapter 6).

Definition of key-terms

Mission – This refers primarily to the *missio Dei* (God's mission).[1]

Missions – This "refers to particular forms, related to specific times, places, or needs, of participation in the *missio Dei*."[2]

Missiology – This is "the systematic and academic study of missions in the fulfillment of God's mission."[3]

Diaspora missiology – This is "a missiological framework for understanding and participating in God's redemptive mission among diaspora groups."[4]

Diaspora missions – This is "Christians' participation in God's redemptive mission to evangelize their kinsmen on the move, and through them to reach out to natives in their homelands and beyond."[5]

Relational paradigm – Theologically, this is "grounded on the fact that man was created in the image of God and his existence (ontologically) is solely dependent on God at all times... His ability to know (epistemologically) and his undertaking in mission (*missio Dei*) are all dependent on God, Who is the great 'I AM.'"[6]

Cross-cultural ministry – Christian ministry to serve people not from one's own ethnic/cultural group.

Chinese churches – Churches that mainly serve first-generation Chinese and their families. These churches may have English ministries to serve second-generation Chinese and Chinese who grew up in the U.S.

Xenophobia – The fear of another culture due to various causes and may lead to racism, hate groups, and crime.[7]

Ethnocentrism – The belief that one's culture, race, or ethnicity is the best and may lead to bigotry and intolerance of others who are different.[8]

---

[1] David J. Bosch, *Transforming Mission: Paradigm Shifts in Theology of Mission*, (Maryknoll, NY: Orbis Books, 2012), 10.

[2] Bosch, 10.

[3] Enoch Wan, *Diaspora Missiology: Theory, Methodology, and Practice*, (Portland, OR: Institute of Diaspora Studies – US, 2011), 6.

[4] Wan, *Diaspora Missiology: Theory, Methodology, and Practice*, 5.

[5] Wan, *Diaspora Missiology: Theory, Methodology, and Practice*, 5.

[6] Wan, *Diaspora Missiology: Theory, Methodology, and Practice*, 143.

[7] Patty Lane, *A Beginner's Guide to Crossing Cultures: Making Friends in a Multicultural World*, (Downers Grove, IL: InterVarsity Press, 2002), 37.

[8] Lane, 38.

Evangelical – Those who emphasize 1) conversion, the belief that lives need to be changed through a personal relationship with Christ, 2) activism, doing evangelism and missionary work for the gospel, 3) Biblicism, emphasizing the importance of the Bible, and 4) "crucicentrism," making central the atoning sacrifice of Christ on the cross.[9]

Methods of data collection

Qualitative study

In *Qualitative Research Practice: A Guide for Social Science Students and Researchers,*[10] Dawn Snape and Liz Spencer quoted the following definition for qualitative research given by Denzin and Lincoln in the second edition of their *Handbook of Qualitative Research*:

Qualitative research is a situated activity that locates the observer in the world. It consists of a set of interpretive, material practices that makes the world visible. These practices ... turn the world into a series of representations including fieldnotes, interviews, conversations, photographs, recordings, and memos to the self. At this level, qualitative research involves an interpretive, naturalistic approach to the world. This means that qualitative researchers study things in their natural settings, attempting to make sense of, or to interpret, phenomena in terms of the meanings people bring to them.[11]

The two case studies were qualitative study since they included interviews, conversations, and recordings. The interviews were conducted by co-author Lei in person and by email with Pastor Joe (Ark Baptist Church) and over the phone and by email with Elder Jupin (Forerunner Christian Church). The interviews included both verbal conversations and email exchanges. The recordings included recording the phone conversation with Elder Jupin. After the call, Lei transcribed the phone conversation recording. He then organized the interview transcript for Elder Jupin to review and edit. The responses from Pastor Joe (Ark Baptist Church) and Elder Jupin (Forerunner Christian Church) were also in the form of emails and Word document.

---

[9] A. Scott Moreau, *Contextualization in World Missions: Mapping and Assessing Evangelical Models,* (Grand Rapids, MI: Kregel, 2012), 19.
[10] Dawn Snape and Liz Spencer, in Jane Ritchie and Jane Lewis, eds., *Qualitative Research Practice: A Guide for Social Science Students and Researchers,* (London: Sage Publications, 2003), 2-3.
[11] N.K. Denzin and Y.S. Lincoln, eds., *Handbook of Qualitative Research,* 2nd ed. (Thousand Oaks, CA: Sage, 2000), 3.

Archival research

Louise Corti's SAGE encyclopedia defines archival research as "the locating, evaluating, and systematic interpretation and analysis of sources found in archives."[12] SAGE dictionary defines archival research as "research that involves review of records or documents in archives."[13]

For the archival research, co-author Lei referenced the latest books and articles on diaspora missions, Chinese diaspora, Chinese diaspora in the SFBA, demographics of the SFBA, and cross-cultural training. This included internet research of church websites of Chinese churches in the SFBA. Archival research was conducted through Internet research using the church websites of Chinese churches in the SFBA to see if 1) they had an English ministry, and 2) they had any local ministries which may be cross-cultural. Data were also collected on how the church was started.

Data Collection: Data were collected through archival research of the websites of churches listed in *The Bay Area Chinese Churches Research Project Phase II*. For each church website, data were collected according to the following questions and coded to more specific categories:

1. How was the church started?
2. Is there English worship? (Yes/No)
3. Is there English or bilingual website? (Yes/No)
4. What types of local cross-cultural ministry are mentioned?
5. Data analysis: The archival research was analyzed to find common themes and threads in Chinese church history and local cross-cultural ministries in the SFBA.
6. Based on the four main questions and sub-category questions, the results were compiled to show how Chinese churches in the SFBA were started, what percentage of Chinese churches in the SFBA had English or bilingual websites, what was the percentage of Chinese churches in the SFBA that had English worship, and what were the local cross-cultural ministries mentioned.

The purpose of the archival research was to research local cross-cultural ministries of Chinese churches in the SFBA. Internet searches were used to find church websites and look for any mention of local ministries that may be cross-cultural. This included searching for English ministries, and for local ministries which served or reached people who were not Chinese. Data were also collected on how the church was started.

---

[12] Louise Corti, "Archival Research," <http://srmo.sagepub.com/view/the-sage-encyclopedia-of-social-science-research-methods/n20.xml> (4/18/2016).
[13] SAGE Knowledge. Dictionary entry for "Archival Research," class handout from Western Seminary DIS725, Spring 2015.

For the archival study, co-author Lei conducted internet research of the websites of Chinese churches in the SFBA, according to the churches listed in *The Bay Area Chinese Churches Research Project Phase II*. The author looked for cross-cultural ministries mentioned on the websites of Chinese churches in the SFBA. The internet research was conducted to see 1) if they had an English ministry, 2) if they had any local ministries which may be cross-cultural. The archival research also looked at the history of how these churches were planted from church websites and *The Bay Area Chinese Churches Research Project Phase II* report. *The Bay Area Chinese Churches Research Project Phase II* reported that 83.5% of the churches listed had websites.[14] *The Bay Area Chinese Churches Research Project Phase II* research also involved accessing the church websites.[15]

Archival research of the SFBA Chinese diaspora churches was mainly from internet websites and did not include church documents, reports, or interviews. The study attempted to contextualize diaspora missions and local cross–cultural ministry to Chinese diaspora churches in the SFBA by offering relevant information and suggestions though not a full curriculum.

Internet research

This study includes internet research, a recent research phenomenon which is developing rapidly.[16] However, one of the biggest challenges that online researchers face is the ethical and legal complexity of the internet.[17] There are introductions to the area of online research methods: *The Internet Handbook* (O'Dochartaigh 2001), *Internet Research Methods* (Hewson, Yule, Laurent, and Vogel 2002), and *Online Research Essential* (Russell and Purcell 2009).[18] In the *SAGE Handbook of Online Research Methods*, there is a section on "The internet as an archival resource," with chapters on "The Provision of Access to Quantitative Data for Secondary Analysis" and "Secondary Qualitative Analysis Using Internet Resources."[19] This study used internet research as primary research by analyzing the data collected from the church websites. Internet research was also used in the Ark Baptist Church case study for church history and vision.

---

[14] James Chuck and Timothy Tseng, eds., *The 2008 Report: The Bay Area Chinese Churches Research Project Phase II*, (Castro Valley: ISAAC, 2009), 4.
<http://www.chinesecommunityumc.org/docs/File%20for%20the%202008%20REPORT.pdf> (February 17, 2013).
[15] Chuck and Tseng, 1.
[16] Tristram Hooley, John Marriott, and Jane Wellens, *What is Online Research? Using the Internet for Social Science Research*, (New York, NY: Bloomsbury Academic, 2012), 7.
[17] Hooley, Marriott, and Wellens, 3.
[18] Hooley, Marriott, and Wellens, 5.
[19] Nigel Fielding, Raymond M. Lee, and Grant Blank. *The SAGE Handbook of Online Research Methods* (Los Angeles, CA: SAGE Publishing, 2008), vi.

Case Study

Case study research is "a qualitative approach in which the investigator explores a real-life, contemporary bounded system (a *case*) or multiple bounded systems (cases) over time, through detailed, in-depth data collection involving *multiple sources of information* (e.g., observations, interviews, audiovisual material, and documents and reports), and reports a *case description* and *case themes.*"[20]

Robert K. Yin sees a case study as an empirical inquiry that "investigates a contemporary phenomenon within its real-life context."[21] Robert E. Stake ("Case Studies," in Norman K. Denzin and Yvonna S. Lincoln, eds., *Handbook of Qualitative Research*) sees that case study can be both qualitative and quantitative.

The case studies were based on interviews with Pastor Joe (Ark Baptist Church) and Elder Jupin (Forerunner Christian Church). The studies included interviews and website documentation (Ark Baptist Church). The first church chosen for study was Ark Baptist Church. This church is co-author Lei's local home church. The pastor of Ark Baptist Church, Pastor Joe, was interviewed for the case study. He also helped to review Lei's translation of the church history and "1312 vision." Pastor Joe met with Lei in person for discussion regarding the case study and to answer follow-up question #1 "What are other ministries or activities that serve/include non-Chinese people?" In addition he gave responses to Lei's questions #2 "What do you see are the challenges of local cross-cultural ministries?" and #3 "What do you see the church doing in local cross-cultural ministries in the near and distant future?" by Word document via email.

The second church chosen for case study was Forerunner Christian Church. In co-author Lei's internet website research, he noticed Forerunner Christian Church mentioned on their church website several local cross-cultural community outreach activities and partnership with a well-known mission organization to engage in local outreach. After an introduction from Pastor Joe to connect with a coworker from Forerunner Christian Church, Lei was referred by the Senior Pastor Grace to Elder Jupin. Interviews with Elder Jupin were conducted on the phone in two phone conversations. This included the "History of local cross-cultural ministries at Forerunner Christian Church," and the follow-up questions: #2 "What do you see are the challenges of local cross-cultural ministries?" and #3 "What do you see the church doing in local cross-cultural ministries in the near and distant future?" Lei then emailed the transcripts of the phone interviews to Elder Jupin for her review and editing. The first follow-up question #1 "What are other ministries or activities that

---

[20] Fielding, Lee, and Blank., 97.
[21] Robert K. Yin, *Case Study Research: Design and Methods*, 2nd ed. (Thousand Oaks, CA: Sage Publications, 1994), 13.

serve/include non-Chinese people? i.e. community service, outreaches, programs, sports, social events, neighborhood events, etc.," was answered by Elder Jupin through email. The case study interviews with Elder Jupin were edited by both Elder Jupin and Lei.

Ethnographic field research

The following is from *A Synthesis of Ethnographic Research*, by Michael Genzuk, Ph.D., Center for Multilingual, Multicultural Research, University of Southern California:

Ethnography is a social science research method. It relies heavily on up-close, personal experience and possible participation, not just observation, by researchers trained in the art of ethnography. These ethnographers often work in multidisciplinary teams. The ethnographic focal point may include intensive language and culture learning, intensive study of a single field or domain, and a blend of historical, observational, and interview methods. Typical ethnographic research employs three kinds of data collection: interviews, observation, and documents. This in turn produces three kinds of data: quotations, descriptions, and excerpts of documents, resulting in one product: narrative description.[22]

The two case studies are also ethnographic field research. This includes interviews, observation, and documents. Through the interviews, co-author Lei made observations. In the first case study, since Ark Baptist Church is Lei's local home church, he made observations of the local cross-cultural ministries mentioned. Pastor Joe (Ark Baptist Church) gave a written quotation narrative in his answers to follow-up questions #2 and #3. The first phone interview with Elder Jupin produced a quotation narrative of the story behind the Forerunner Christian Church's local cross-cultural ministries. The second phone interview with Elder Jupin produced quotation narratives of follow-up question #2 "What do you see are the challenges of local cross-cultural ministries?" and follow-up question #3 "What do you see the church doing in local cross-cultural ministries in the near and distant future?"

---

[22] Michael Genzuk, *A Synthesis of Ethnographic Research*, (Center for Multilingual, Multicultural Research, University of Southern California, 2003).

CHAPTER 2
HISTORICAL STUDY OF CHINESE DIASPORA AND CHINESE DIASPORA CHURCHES IN THE SAN FRANCISCO BAY AREA

History of Chinese Diaspora to North America

Chinese people began immigrating to North America from China prior to the 14th Century. There was an acceleration of emigration from China in the early 19th Century due to the push effect of population explosion, famines, political instability, and other factors, and the pull effect of better life and more opportunities abroad.[23] Between 1850 and 1882, over 322,000 Chinese, especially the Cantonese from Guangdong Province, came to the United States.[24] Prior to 1849, there were not many Chinese in the U.S. Michael Stahler writes, "Only three Chinese lived in San Francisco in 1848. By 1849 the number increased to 700, with most being importers and jobbers."[25] The discovery of gold and jobs attracted many Chinese to California, the Pacific Northwest, and British Columbia.[26]

An influx of Chinese immigration occurred during the 1850s. Sudhanshu Bhandari writes, "The real surge in Chinese immigration from Guangdong Province to California took place in the year 1852, when as per the San

---

[23] Enoch Wan, "Mission Among the Chinese Diaspora – A Case Study of Migration and Mission." <http://www.enochwan.com/english/articles/pdf/Mission%20among%20the%20Chinese%20Dia spora.pdf> (February 17, 2013).
[24] Wesley Woo, "Presbyterian Mission: Christianizing and Civilizing the Chinese in Nineteenth Century California," *American Presbyterians*, 68:3 (Fall 1990), 167.
[25] Michael L. Stahler, "William Speer: Champion of California's Chinese, 1852-1857," *Journal of Presbyterian History*, 48 (Summer 1970), 113.
[26] Sucheng Chan, *Asian Americans: An Interpretive History*, (Boston: Twayne Publishers, 1991), 3.

Francisco custom-house figures, 20,026 Chinese labourers arrived on the shores of America."[27] The previous year in 1851, only 2,716 Chinese had arrived.[28] Bhandari reports, "Statistical information relating to overseas immigration in the US available from 1820 shows that during the period 1820-1850, hardly 800 Chinese had arrived, of which 775 had arrived in the years 1849 and 1850 itself."[29]

The population of Chinese in America peaked in 1890, with 107,488 Chinese reported to be in the country.[30] However, the 1882 Chinese Exclusion Act and other anti-Chinese measures lead to a decline in the population after this period.[31]

World War II changed the attitude of Americans towards the Chinese. Sucheng Chan writes that a Gallup poll taken in 1942 shows the American respondents characterized the Chinese as "hardworking, honest, brave, religious, intelligent, and practical."[32] This poll reflects how newspapers covering the war in Asia were sympathetic to the Chinese.[33]

There were about 5,000 Chinese college and graduate students studying in the Unites States when a Communist government came to power in China in 1949. These students were granted political asylum which allowed these Chinese intellectuals to remain in the country.[34] Chan writes, "These men and women sought work in universities, research laboratories, and private industries, bought homes in the suburbs, and had little to do with the old-time Chinese immigrants except for occasional meals in and shopping trips to the various Chinatowns of America."[35]

There were 3,000 Chinese refugees who came under the 1953 Refugee Act and acts passed in 1957 and 1959.[36] A presidential directive signed by John F. Kennedy in 1962 allowed another 15,000 to come into the country.[37] Chan writes, "The influx of some 23,000 highly educated and well-trained Chinese refugees greatly augmented the ranks of the Chinese American middle class."[38] Many Chinese students came to the United States in the 1960s.[39] Since 1965, the

---

[27] Sudhanshu Bhandari, "Discrimination and Perseverance Amongst the Chinese in California in the Nineteenth and Early-Twentieth Centuries," *China Report*, 47:1 (February 2011), 4-5.
[28] Bhandari, 4-5.
[29] Bhandari, 4-5.
[30] Woo, "Presbyterian Mission," 167.
[31] Woo, "Presbyterian Mission," 167.
[32] Chan, 121.
[33] Chan, 121.
[34] Chan, 141.
[35] Chan, 141.
[36] Chan, 141.
[37] Chan, 141.
[38] Chan, 141.
[39] Ronald Takak, *A History of Asian Americans: Strangers from a Different Shore*, (New York: Back Bay Books, 1998), 422.

number of Chinese quota immigrants from PRC and ROC combined has been about 460,000, and the combined non-quota immigrants were approximately 15,000 for the same period.[40]

Here are some events related to the Chinese diaspora in America from Sucheng Chan's *Asian Americans: An Interpretive History*:[41]

1600s – Chinese and Filipinos sailors reach Mexico.[42]

1830s – Chinese "sugar masters" working in Hawaii; Chinese sailors and peddlers arrive in New York.[43]

1844 – First treaty between United States and China.[44]

1848 – Chinese arrive after discovery of gold in California.[45]

1857 – In San Francisco, a school is opened for Chinese children; missionary Augustus Loomis arrives to serve the Chinese.[46]

1865 – "Central Pacific Railroad Co. recruits Chinese workers for the first transcontinental railroad."[47]

1882 – The Chinese Exclusion Act bans Chinese laborer immigration for ten years.[48]

1902 – The Chinese Exclusion Act is extended for ten more years.[49]

1904 – The Chinese Exclusion Act is made permanent and applies to U.S. insular territories.[50]

1949 – "Five thousand highly educated Chinese in the United States are granted refugee status after a Communist government comes to power in China."[51]

1965 – Immigration law abolishes "national origins" based immigration quotas for various countries.[52]

1979 – Diplomatic relations resumed between the People's Republic of China and the United States allowing "members of long-separated Chinese American families to be reunited."[53]

History of Chinese Diaspora to California

---

[40] Chan, 151.
[41] Chan, 192-199.
[42] Chan, 192.
[43] Chan, 192.
[44] Chan, 192.
[45] Chan, 192.
[46] Chan, 192.
[47] Chan, 192.
[48] Chan, 193.
[49] Chan, 194.
[50] Chan, 195.
[51] Chan, 197.
[52] Chan, 198.
[53] Chan, 198.

Early Chinese immigrants came to California in the 1850s. They worked as gardeners, railroad builders, highway builders, fishermen, and miners. The Chinese lived in the areas from Monterey Bay to Santa Clara Country in the south to San Francisco Bay in the north. On a wall mural in Monterey Bay, an inscription reads:

> In 1879, the population of Pacific Grove's Chinatown was nearly 70 men, women and children. Within this makeshift village, located where Hopkins Marine Station now stands, the Chinese practiced their traditions and developed the techniques of nighttime squid fishing. In 1906, a mysterious and tragic fire destroyed most of the village. The last Chinese disappeared from the village in 1907.[54]

In 1887, it is recorded that in San Jose a Chinatown burned down. Since the 1860s the Chinese have lived in Gilroy, Milpitas, Alviso, Campbell, Cupertino, and Mountain View.[55]

From the 1940s to 1960s, Chinese people with better education came to California. Unlike the earlier Chinese blue-collar laborers, these highly educated Chinese were able to move into the middle class. They worked as professors, doctors, and dentists, and were the distinguished members of the Asian community in the Silicon Valley.[56]

Bernard Wong sees five tech-related waves of foreign-born Chinese migration to California from the 1950s to 2000. The first wave of Chinese technology immigrants was sponsored by IBM and other American companies in the 1950s. The second wave of Chinese immigrants arrived in the 1960s to work for defense industries. The third wave was related to the graduate students from mainland China after 1970, when PRC relaxed its policies for studying in the United States. The fourth wave of immigrants came from within the United States, Taiwan, mainland China, and other overseas Chinese communities in the late 1980s and 1990s. The fifth wave of immigrants came during 1990 to 2000 and was generally mainland Chinese students who finished their graduate training in the United States and found employment in the Silicon Valley.[57] Co-author Lei himself moved from Texas to the Silicon Valley in 2009 for employment reasons.

Missionary Efforts to Early Chinese

---

[54] Painted Wall Mural on Ocean View Blvd, Pacific Grove, CA. Seen by author July 9, 2013.
[55] Wong, *The Chinese in Silicon Valley: Globalization, Social Networks, and Ethnic Identity*, (Lanham, MD: Rowan & Littlefield Publishers, Inc., 2006), 19.
[56] Bernard P. Wong, 20.
[57] Bernard P. Wong, 21.

Settlers

In the 1850s the only education that children of Chinese ancestry could obtain was from private tutors hired by their parents or from English and Bible classes taught by Protestant missionaries working in Chinatown.[58] This leads us to the discussion about Presbyterian missionary work that began in San Francisco in the early 1850s.

For centuries, Christian missionaries went to China to spread the gospel. With the influx of Chinese from 1849, there was now an opportunity to evangelize the Chinese in the United States. The Presbyterian Board of Foreign Missions received requests from members in California to start a local mission ministry to the Chinese.[59] They also saw the opportunity for Chinese Christians to return to China as Christian missionaries, since they had observed that Chinese people regularly return to China.[60] In 1852, the Presbyterian Board of Foreign Missions appointed William Speer and his wife to open a mission among the Chinese in California.[61]

Others started reaching out to Chinese in San Francisco. Reverend Albert Williams of First Presbyterian Church of San Francisco and Mayor John W. Geary spoke to 100 Chinese at Portsmouth Plaza on October 20, 1850. They also distributed religious books and tracts to the Chinese.[62]

Speer did not gain many converts in the five years from 1852-1857. Stahler writes, "One contemporary of Speer reported that only one Oriental was baptized at the mission, a man named Young Fo, who later became a colporteur for the American Tract Society."[63] Another person who studied this subject gave Speer credit for gaining no more than six members in the Chinese Presbyterian Church.[64]

Stahler sees the low conversion rate was due to Speer's own strict standards for conversion. The candidates for conversion needed to have a testimony of their faith, obtain a full understanding of the Old and New Testament and several months of probation before baptism was performed.[65] However, Speer is credited for his humanitarian work to fight for the better treatment of Chinese people.

Another Christian mission work in San Francisco helped Chinese women who were involved in prostitution and caught in the sex trade. Iris Chang writes, "By the 1870s, horrified Christian activists, mostly middle-class white

---

[58] Bernard P. Wong, 57.
[59] Stahler, 114.
[60] Stahler, 114.
[61] Stahler, 114.
[62] Stahler, 115.
[63] Stahler, 117.
[64] Stahler, 117.
[65] Stahler, 117.

Protestant women, established rescue homes for Chinese women." [66] There were two such sanctuaries in San Francisco: the Women's Missionary Society of the Methodist Episcopal Church was established by Reverend Otis Gibson; the Presbyterian Mission Home was founded by the Woman's Occidental Board.[67]

The mission homes tried to protect the women who came to them. They hid them from the criminals who came looking for them. These mission homes experienced harassment from the criminals who engaged in the sex trade.[68] Christian workers such as Donaldine Cameron, director of the Presbyterian Mission Home, heroically stood up to these criminals. Chang sees that "these efforts drew considerable press attention to Chinatown's criminal element and greatly contributed to the demise of Chinese prostitution on the West Coast.[69]

History of Chinese Christian Communities and Churches in North America

In *The "Chinese" Way of Doing Things*, Samuel Ling traced the history of Chinese Christian Communities in North America. Ling starts by describing the influence of American missionaries who went to China in the nineteenth century. He writes, "Most of the American missionaries who went to China came from the post-revolutionary, nineteenth century rural context of the American heartland. In the small community, there was a down-home atmosphere, an emphasis on relationships, and a common man attitude which was suspicious of the intellectual elite of the East Coast."[70] This influence led to an anti-intellectual tradition in the Chinese church. Also, the anti-missionary, anti-foreign sentiments in China led to a tradition of isolation in the church.[71] This anti-intellectual and tradition of isolation would become a problem when Chinese churches begin to be filled with intellectuals in the twentieth century. Ling points to the challenge of discipling Chinese intellectuals "to impact culture without being secularized by the culture in the process."[72]

Not all of the American missionaries were anti-intellectual, especially those in the Mainline denominations. By the 1880s, these missionaries had started

---

[66] Iris Chang, *The Chinese in America: A Narrative History*, (New York: Viking, 2003), 85.
[67] Chang, 85.
[68] Chang, 86.
[69] Chang, 86.
[70] Samuel Ling with Clarence Cheuk, *The "Chinese" Way of Doing Things: Perspectives on American-Born Chinese and the Chinese Church in North America*, (Vancouver, Canada: Horizon Ministries Canada, 1999), 90.
[71] Ling and Cheuk, 90-91.
[72] Ling and Cheuk, 91.

colleges and universities. Ling writes, "In the first half of the twentieth century, there were over a dozen Protestant universities in China, such as Yenching in Beijing, Cheeloo in Shantung, St. John's in Shanghai, Soochow University, and Lingnan in Guanzhou."[73]

Many of these graduates from China came to North America and stayed in the U.S. during the Korean War. They became the first generation of Chinese professionals in North America. However, the liberal Protestant education they received left them largely secularized.[74]

More Chinese students came to North America in the 1960s and 1970s. Chinese Christian students started Bible study groups and Christian fellowships. These groups were mostly independent from any denomination or student movement such as InterVarsity, Campus Crusade, and The Navigators.[75] Ling notes, "This independence was borrowed from the fundamentalist spirituality of the church in China, Taiwan, and Hong Kong."[76] While many of these Chinese Christians did not become members in local churches, they were starting to form their own congregations in the 1980s and 1990s.[77]

Samuel Ling sees three phases in the development of the Chinese church in North America in the second half of the twentieth century: 1) the shaping of a community (1943-1963), 2) institutionalization of the Chinese church (1963-1979),[78] and 3) the Computer Age (1980—present)."[79]

The first phase in the development of the Chinese church in North America began in 1943 with the repeal of the Chinese Exclusionary Act, which resumed Chinese immigration to America. As the U.S. moved into the 1950s, it experienced great technological advances, along with an increase of Chinese immigration to America. This increasing immigration lead to a "floodtide" in the 1960s and 1970s.[80] During the Korean War, Chinese-Americans were given scholarships and many became doctors, diplomats, and other professionals. Children born into these families became American-born Chinese. The Chinese community in America grew more divergent as more Chinese entered into professional fields. Ling notes, "A two-part Chinese community thus took shape: immigrant and student, worker and professional, urban and suburban, struggling and successful."[81]

During this period, Protestant denominations in North America supported "home missions work among the Chinese in large cities – San Francisco, Los

---

[73] Ling and Cheuk, 91.
[74] Ling and Cheuk, 92.
[75] Ling and Cheuk, 92.
[76] Ling and Cheuk, 92.
[77] Ling and Cheuk, 92.
[78] Ling and Cheuk, 95.
[79] Ling and Cheuk, 100.
[80] Ling and Cheuk, 94.
[81] Ling and Cheuk, 94.

Angeles, Chicago, New York, Philadelphia, and so forth."[82] This home mission's work included Sunday school classes for Chinese children and English and Bible classes for Chinese women. Females from the laity made up most of the workers in this missions work.[83]

Chinese Christian students also started to organize their own conferences. In 1957, one hundred Chinese students met at a summer conference in York, Pennsylvania. The Ambassadors magazine was launched from this conference. Later this magazine was published by Ambassadors for Christ, a Chinese mission organization founded in 1963 in Washington D.C. The Chinese Christian Mission, a mass evangelism ministry was founded by Thomas Wang in 1961. Evangelists Moses Yu and Calvin Chao also started student ministries which developed into churches.[84] Ling notes the "pattern of para-church organizations, serving the Chinese church and planting new ones, was now set."[85]

Many of the students and immigrants experienced "culture shock" when they first came to the U.S. Through the outreach of the Chinese Christian community, these people responded to the gospel of Jesus Christ. They were nurtured in the local churches and student fellowships and grew in zeal and piety in the Christian faith. Their passion for the Christian faith contributed to the growth of Chinese Christian churches and ministries. Ling sees that this "provided a foundation upon which later ministries were to build from."[86]

Co-author Lei himself responded to the gospel in college through the outreach activities of a local Chinese church. He was also facing a new environment in college at the time and the Chinese church provided the warmth and support of a Chinese Christian community. The positive nurturing environment in the Chinese church as well as InterVarsity on campus contributed to the spiritual growth of Lei in his early years as a Christian.

The second phase in the development of the Chinese church in North America began in 1963. Samuel Ling titles 1963-1979 as "the Death of Christian Civilization and the Institutionalization of the Chinese Church (1963-1979)."[87] During this time, the Christian culture in America was being challenged by the Vietnam War protests, antiwar movement, energy crisis, and the pursuit of personal financial security.[88] In China, the Cultural Revolution was removing all traditional and religious influences. Ling writes of this period, "Traditional Christian civilization, along with values which emphasize the dignity of

---

[82] Ling and Cheuk, 94.
[83] Ling and Cheuk, 94.
[84] Ling and Cheuk, 94.
[85] Ling and Cheuk, 94-95.
[86] Ling and Cheuk, 95.
[87] Ling and Cheuk, 95.
[88] Ling and Cheuk, 95-96.

humanity and the importance of family and community, crumbled before our eyes."[89]

Following the Kennedy Act in 1965, which increased the quota of immigrants from outside the Western Hemisphere, Chinese immigrated to America by the thousands. Many Chinese families, workers, and students found homes in the cities of America.[90] At the same time, American-born children of the Chinese students from the Korean War era grew up and changed the profile of the Chinese community.[91]

Chinese Christian students who came in the 1960s and 1970s formed Chinese Bible study groups (CBSGs) or Chinese Christian Fellowships (CCFs).[92] Ling notes that this "was a unique phenomenon among all the foreign students in North America during this period; no other group of foreign students formed as many spontaneous, student-run and independent Christian fellowships as the Chinese."[93] These Chinese students gained a variety of skills in the U.S. and leveraged these skills for evangelistic outreach and discipleship. Others used their financial resources to support seminary students or for evangelistic causes.[94]

During this period, Chinese churches were planted in great numbers. Ling writes, "Many graduates from universities and graduate schools started their own churches; some of these churches were little more than extensions of existing student-run CBSGs or CCFs."[95] However, other churches were started "because of interpersonal communication breakdowns and power struggles."[96] Ling notes that these two types of churches "comprised a very significant proportion of the total of Chinese churches in North America."[97]

In these years, the number of American-raised Chinese who grew up in the suburbs increased. These young people entered prestigious schools and were influential and successful in their career fields, and they also dropped out of church after entering college.[98]

Another group that immigrated to the U.S. during this time is the immigrant pastors and their families who served in the Chinese churches. They also experienced "culture shock" after coming to the U.S. However, Ling notes that those "who immigrated in the 1980s and 1990s seem to have less difficulties in adjustment, having lived through Taipei's and Hong Kong's transition to global

---

[89] Ling and Cheuk, 96.
[90] Ling and Cheuk, 96.
[91] Ling and Cheuk, 96.
[92] Ling and Cheuk, 96.
[93] Ling and Cheuk, 96-97.
[94] Ling and Cheuk, 97-98.
[95] Ling and Cheuk, 98.
[96] Ling and Cheuk, 98.
[97] Ling and Cheuk, 98.
[98] Ling and Cheuk, 98.

cities."[99] These immigrant Chinese pastors used Asian models of church ministry and were most effective in ministering to the first-generation Chinese immigrant believers.[100]

Many Chinese students attended Urbana, InterVarsity's triennial missionary convention held at the University of Illinois. One Chinese mission organization started from attendees at the Urbana conference is the Chinese Coordination Centre of World Evangelism (CCCOWE). Ling details the history of CCCOWE:

> Some of these pastors gathered at Urbana 1970 and planned the North America Congress of Chinese Evangelicals (NACOCE), which was held in December 1972. The West Coast Chinese Christian Students Winter Conference cancelled their 1972 conference and contributed local manpower toward NACOCE's on-site operation. NACOCE was held subsequently at Wheaton, Illinois (1974), Toronto, Canada (1978), Pasadena, California (1979), and Chicago (1983). After 1986, NACOCE was renamed Chinese Coordination Centre of World Evangelism-North America (CCCOWE-NA). Today it is known as two entities: CCCOWE-USA and CCCOWE-Canada.[101]

Co-author Lei himself attended Urbana 2000 and Urbana 2003, which deeply impacted him and gave him an interest in world missions.

Ling designates the third phase in the development of the Chinese church in North America as "The Computer Age (1980—present)."[102] By this time, the Chinese immigrants were becoming more diverse. Many went to the large cities in North America, including Chinese immigrants from People's Republic of China, Singapore, and Malaysia. Many restaurant workers moved from Chinatown to other areas. Ling notes, "Chinese were by no means assimilated into American society, but they were more evenly distributed across the North American landscape."[103]

In the 1980s and 1990s American Chinese were becoming more acceptable as being Chinese or Asian. They were becoming the "envy of other minorities in America."[104]

Samuel Ling, however, saw the prosperity and success of Chinese Christians in North America did not help them relate the gospel to their surrounding communities.[105] Ling notes the "time-honored model of 'rejection and denial of culture' persisted, and those who sought to go beyond this mostly reached a

---

[99] Ling and Cheuk, 99.
[100] Ling and Cheuk, 99.
[101] Ling and Cheuk, 99.
[102] Ling and Cheuk, 100.
[103] Ling and Cheuk, 101.
[104] Ling and Cheuk, 102.
[105] Ling and Cheuk, 100.

stage of 'juxtaposition of Christianity with secular culture.'"[106] This began to change in the 1990s when American ministries such as Promise Keepers and Focus on the Family started to have an impact on Chinese Christians in North America.[107] Co-author Lei agrees with Ling's observation. Lei had attended the Promise Keepers conference with members of the Chinese congregation who had organized the trip. Lei has also seen books by Focus on the Family founder Dr. James Dobson translated into Chinese and read by people in the Chinese congregation. While in the Bay Area, Lei also saw an increasing interest from Chinese pastors to be involved in the community and to transform the community for Christ.

With the growth and success of Chinese churches in North America, there is still the issue of how Chinese churches can serve the American-born Chinese (ABC). Ling points to the problem of ABC pastors dropping out of the Chinese church or being unable to find employment. He writes, "Among the American-born Chinese Christians, many seminary graduates are unemployed, unable to fulfill the Chinese churches' requirement that they speak Chinese."[108]

Gail Law also describes the difficulty of integrating ABC into the Chinese churches. He writes:

> The 1980 U.S. census shows that about 40% of the Chinese in America were ABC, but in the Chinese churches only 22.4% attended the English-speaking services. This figure included both ABCs and those OBCs who, for various reasons, preferred the English to the Chinese services. Few ABCs were represented on the church boards and even fewer made it to the pastorate, despite the fact that some of them did acquire the formal theological training.[109]

Seminaries are recognizing the need to train workers to more effectively minister in Chinese churches. Ling writes, "In the 1980s, several evangelical seminaries began to offer courses, majors, and degree programs within their traditional curriculum structure to meet the need of culturally sensitive Chinese pastors in North America." [110] These seminaries seek to address the issues and concerns of Asia-born Chinese as well as provide in-depth study of the Chinese culture.[111]

---

[106] Ling and Cheuk, 100.
[107] Ling and Cheuk, 100.
[108] Ling and Cheuk, 102.
[109] Gail Law, "A Model for the American Ethnic Chinese Churches," in Cecilia Yau, ed. *A Winning Combination: ABC/OBC* (Petaluma, CA: Chinese Christian Mission, 1986), 131.
[110] Ling and Cheuk, 103.
[111] Ling and Cheuk, 103.

Socio-cultural Profile/Characteristics

The Chinese immigrant community can vary widely. Vinod C. Khanna quotes from Wang Gungwu to show the importance of culture and history in the formation of Chinese immigrant communities:

> Culture and history do matter in the way migrant communities are formed and evolved. It is not enough to say that Chinese immigrants are industrious, practice thrift and make sacrifices for their families, value education and social mobility, and organize themselves for effective defense and action...When the Chinese left home and where they went to played extremely important parts in shaping the communities they formed outside China.[112]

I-Shu Huang points out that traditional Chinese ethics is against leaving the homeland and settling down in faraway places. She quotes the Confucian saying: "Don't you travel when your parents are alive" (fumuzai bu yuanyou).[113] However, Huang notes the paradox that "the Chinese are one of the largest diaspora communities today."[114] She observes that "almost every Chinese diaspora is determined not to go back before achieving success of sorts."[115]

Huang sees three common traits of the Chinese diaspora. The first trait is their hardworking nature.[116] The second trait is the China-oriented unity and fellowship among the overseas Chinese in friendship, partnership and collaboration in careers, enterprises and investments, and social life.[117] The third trait is harmony. Huang writes, "'He wei gui' (peace is treasurable) is a value shared by most Chinese diaspora. They treasure harmony because they have paid heavily to get the chance of living abroad."[118] The Chinese diaspora tend to avoid political involvement and be silent even when they encounter anti-Chinese injustices and choose to be law-abiding and authority-fearing.[119] However, the Chinese diaspora may become more vocal now that China is becoming a major world power.

According to Enoch Wan, the Chinese people have the common traits of 1) confrontation avoidance, 2) emphasis on relationship, 3) High-context culture, and 4) honor and shame.[120]

The Chinese culture tries hard to avoid confrontation at all time and at all cost. People try to protect each other from losing face or losing the relationship.

---

[112] Vinod C. Khanna, "The Chinese Diaspora," *China Report*, 37:4 (November 2001), 428-429.
[113] I-Shu Huang, "Culture of the Chinese Diaspora," *China Report*, 37:4 (November 2001), 445.
[114] Huang, 445.
[115] Huang, 445.
[116] Huang, 447.
[117] Huang, 448.
[118] Huang, 448.
[119] Huang, 448.
[120] Wan, "Mission Among the Chinese Diaspora."

The cultural practices such as the use of matchmaking in traditional marriage arrangement, the go-between for business dealing, and the guarantee of a reputable person rather than the signing of a legal document are all related to the culture of protecting people from losing face.[121]

Regarding honor and shame, Wan writes, "To the Chinese, saving face is not just a personal concern but others as well, friends and family included. Honor is more important than personal life, property, and power." [122] Thus, honor and saving face is the life goal of the Chinese. This goal is not only to benefit the individual but also for the benefit of the whole family, including extended family members – living members and even deceased ancestors.[123]

Wan sees the avoidance of shame to self and others built into the whole Chinese cultural system, which includes "individual and group action, social and religious ritual, ceremonial procedures, festival and anniversary, rule of reciprocity and social obligation, giving and receiving gifts, achievement and punishment, law and regulation, etc."[124]

Different Types of Chinese in the Silicon Valley

Bernard Wong lists four types of Chinese in the Silicon Valley. The first type is Chinese Americans who are born in the United States and grew up in the SFBA. The second type is foreign students who have adjusted their visas to stay permanently in America. They have come to the United States since the 1960s and are students from Taiwan and Hong Kong. Their population is concentrated in the Stanford area. The third type is Chinese engineers with advanced degrees who came to the Silicon Valley beginning in the 1980s from Hong Kong, Taiwan, and mainland China. There are also many secondary migrants who moved to the Silicon Valley from other areas of the United States. The fourth type arrived during the 1970s and after 2000 and are from Southeast Asia or a different part of the world.[125] These are the main types of Chinese in the Silicon Valley. There are also others who grew up in the United States and came from other parts of the country. Co-author Lei himself moved from Texas for employment in the Silicon Valley.

Today there are two dominant Chinese ethnic groups in the high-tech industry – the Chinese from Taiwan and those from mainland China.[126] The

---

[121] Wan, "Mission Among the Chinese Diaspora."
[122] Wan, "Mission Among the Chinese Diaspora."
[123] Wan, "Mission Among the Chinese Diaspora."
[124] Wan, "Mission Among the Chinese Diaspora."
[125] Bernard P. Wong, 22.
[126] Bernard P. Wong, 22.

third important ethnic group is from Hong Kong and speaks the Cantonese dialect.[127]

Cultural Differences Among the Diaspora Chinese

Bernard Wong sees three sub-cultures among the mainlanders, the Taiwanese, and those from Hong Kong. Some may call these the *Taiwan Wenhua* (Taiwanese culture), a *Xiang Gen Wenhua* (Hong Kong culture), and a *Da Lu Wenhua* (mainland Chinese culture).[128]

Traits of OBC, ARC, ABC

There are three different types of Chinese American in terms of their level of acculturation or assimilation in the United States and in the Silicon Valley. The first type is the Overseas born Chinese (OBC). They are the first-generation immigrants who were born and raised in China, Taiwan, Hong Kong, and Southeast Asia.[129]

The second type is the American raised Chinese (ARC) who came with their OBC parents usually in their primary school or younger years. Some may have come reluctantly because they had to leave their friends and comfort zone. Even though some came without knowing what to expect, they appreciated their parents for paying such a high price to bring them to the United States to have a better future. They would usually work hard to fulfill the dream their parents had for them. They tend to acculturate faster than the OBC.[130] Co-author Lei himself is an ARC and agrees with Lawrence Fung's observations about the ARC.

The third type is the American born Chinese (ABC). The ABC can be children of OBC or ABC parents. These are more vulnerable to an identity crisis as they grow up. They may either identify more with Chinese culture or with American culture. Or they may react against and reject certain aspects of both cultures.[131] Co-author Lei believes that ARC may also have an identity crisis depending on the age they arrived in the U.S. If at a younger age, they may have similar identity struggles as the ABC.

---

[127] Bernard P. Wong, 23.
[128] Bernard P. Wong, 143.
[129] Lawrence Fung, *A Phenomenological Study of the Role of Pastoral Leadership in Mobilizing Chinese Churches in the San Francisco Bay Area for Global Mission in the 21st Century*, D Miss dissertation, (Western Seminary, Portland, Oregon, 2011), 21.
[130] Fung, 22.
[131] Fung, 23.

The OBC

The OBCs are known for their commitment to the well-being of their families, especially their children, and for the great sacrifices they make to bring their children to the United States or raise their American-born children, so that they may have an opportunity to pursue a brighter future.[132] However, OBCs may operate only in survival mode and have limited contact or appreciation for the America culture. This is especially true in the Silicon Valley where so many Chinese live. They tend to be conservative and traditional and their thinking and lifestyle may be largely unchanged from their native culture even while living in America.[133]

The ARC

Fung writes, "Much of an ARCs' worldview may be contrary to their OBC parents. Partly it is because they tend to be more a "dream catcher" than "dreamer." These work hard in pursuing the American dream that their parents desired for them."[134] ARCs may experience confusion about their own culture: is it Chinese or American? Many ARCs can speak Chinese though may not be able to read or write Chinese. They may prefer to read the English Bible and sing songs in English at church. They may have friends who are Chinese speaking or bilingual. They may have a dual identity, and some have dual citizenship – US and the country of their birth.[135]

Co-author Lei is an ARC, born in Taiwan, and who came to the US when he was in elementary school. During his teenage years, Lei rejected the Chinese language and culture and wanted to be like the other Americans. Lei had almost forgotten how to speak Chinese during his teenage years. It was only when Lei became a Christian in a Chinese church while he was in college that he started to speak Chinese again, however broken it was, because of the need to communicate with the Chinese speaking people at church. Lei remained in the English-speaking youth group and later in the English congregation until years later, when he realized that there are Chinese speaking people he should befriend. This led him to improve his Chinese speaking skills. Later he wanted to have an opportunity to minister to Chinese-speaking people, so he moved to the Chinese congregation and picked up more Chinese reading. However, Lei realized no matter how much he improved his Chinese language skills, he would not have the cultural background of an OBC. He wouldn't be able to relate to them as a fellow OBC, but only as an ARC. To the OBC, he may be seen exactly like an ABC.

---

[132] Fung, 23-24.
[133] Fung, 24.
[134] Fung, 26-27.
[135] Fung, 27.

The ABC

According to Samuel Ling, in the 1970s and 1980s, American-born Chinese sociologists Stanley and Gerald Sue studied the ABC. They found three types of attitudes ABCs have towards traditional Chinese culture.[136] The first type of ABC has a traditional orientation and is comfortable with Chinese language and culture. Some may have spent extended time in China and are conditioned to be comfortable with Chinese language and culture.[137] The second type of ABC rejects the Chinese culture and dislikes their Chinese language school experience. The sociologists found many ABCs born in the 1960s and 1970s have this attitude.[138] The third type of ABC has fully assimilated into American culture and the Chinese culture is not an issue for them because it is not part of their conscious adult life. Many of these ABCs marry non-Chinese and have no need for the Chinese community or Chinatown.[139]

The ABCs born in the '30s and '40s are the first type, their parents are from China and these lived in the Chinatown community. They can be bilingual and see themselves as Chinese. The ABCs born in the '70s and '80s with 2nd or 3rd generation ABC parents are the third type and see themselves as American.[140]

The more conservative and traditional ABCs are more inward, non-involved, and passive in their activities. These can be more family-centered and their activities are more relational. The more Americanized ABCs are more liberal and broad-minded. Their activities can be more outward and involved. They are more individualistic, pragmatic, and goal-oriented.[141]

The ABC with OBC parents may have stronger reactions to the Chinese culture because they feel like they are living with two cultures – Chinese culture at home and American culture at school. This may lead to an "identity crisis" that is above and beyond what is usually normal in typical adolescence. Gail Law sees the differences in Western and Chinese values can cause the ABC to act differently at home and elsewhere. He writes, "At home, an ABC would find much stress on duty, obligation, hierarchy, status, deference, respect, collectivity, self-control, and interdependence. But at school, the teaching emphasizes self-reliance, emotional expression, individual rights, individual privileges, egalitarianism, and self-assertion."[142] The OBC parents may not understand the struggles of the ABC children to live with the two cultures in their life. Law observes, "While most ABCs experience tremendous agony trying to harmonize the two sets of contradicting values which they have imbibed

---

[136] Ling and Cheuk, 118.
[137] Ling and Cheuk, 118.
[138] Ling and Cheuk, 118.
[139] Ling and Cheuk, 119.
[140] Ling and Cheuk, 121.
[141] Ling and Cheuk, 121.
[142] Law, in Cecilia Yau, ed., 133.

since childhood, the OBC parents perceive their ABC children's Americanized behavior as an intrusion into the Chinese heritage."[143]

The ABCs who grow up in Chinatown may be more traditional and not assimilate as well into American culture as the ABCs who grow up in the suburbs, even though those who grow up in the suburbs will still have some degree of "Chinese-ness" inside.[144]

In recent years ABCs have become more interested in their roots and the Chinese culture.[145] The motivation of ABCs varies. Some may want to use it to enhance their careers as China is becoming an economic superpower. There are already many ABCs working in Asia and being well paid for their bilingual Chinese and English abilities.[146] Co-author Lei has also seen among his ABC friends in the SFBA that some are motivated to learn Chinese in order to better their chances in finding a Chinese marriage partner who may be an OBC or who may currently live overseas in Asian countries like China.

Wayland Wong notes, "ABCs are a mixed lot. It is impossible to stereotype an ABC because of the wide spectrum into which they fit. So many different factors influence an ABC's culture that examples could be found from one extreme to the other."[147] Wong proposes using a scale to describe how Chinese and how American an ABC can be. On a scale of 1 to 10 with the very Chinese ABC on the left and the very American ABC on the right, Wong sees that most ABCs would probably fit somewhere in the middle.[148] However, Wong observes that "more and more ABCs are moving to the right, that is, becoming more American by the mere fact that they are of a later generation of ABCs in America."[149]

Wayland Wong lists the factors that will influence an ABC's Chinese-ness or American-ness such as "where he was born, where his parents were born and raised, the culture of his upbringing, his schooling, the kind of church to which he belongs, and how he sees himself."[150]

Che-Bin Tan points to the dramatic change in value system between the second and third generation overseas Chinese through a study in Montreal, Canada (Robert Chin, Montreal Chinese, National Museum of Man, 1975, p.76). In the study, the parents wanted their children "to rank respect to elders and consideration of the elders' needs first, being industrious and studious second, followed by obedience to parents, development of initiative and independent judgment, enjoying life, and, lastly, standing up and fighting for one's right."[151]

---

[143] Law, in Cecilia Yau, ed., 133.
[144] Fung, 29.
[145] Bernard P. Wong, 192.
[146] Bernard P. Wong, 193.
[147] Wayland Wong, "Reaching ABCs...Who Are We Working With?" in Cecilia Yau, ed., 120.
[148] Wayland Wong, in Cecilia Yau, ed., 120.
[149] Wayland Wong, in Cecilia Yau, ed., 120.
[150] Wayland Wong, in Cecilia Yau, ed., 120.
[151] Che Bin Tan, "Chinese Church in Tension Between Two Cultures," in Cecilia Yau, ed., 7.

However, the children ranked development of initiative and independent judgment first, standing up and fighting for one's rights second, followed by being industrious and studious, respect to elders and obedience to parents, and lastly having a good time in life.[152] This study clearly shows the children have basically adopted Western values.[153]

Chinese Cultural Changes

Che-Bin Tan directs attention to a study by H.C. Peng of the Campus Evangelical Fellowship in Taipei that shows Chinese culture is changing in the younger generation. The study was conducted with a group of people, the majority of whom were Christians. This study found that the "older and younger generations value happiness of the whole person and also agreed on the importance of love between different sexes and those within the family."[154]

In addition, the study found the younger generation "did not agree with parents who viewed the family as more important than personal happiness and as the center of activities of all family members."[155] The younger generation also do not accept traditional values such as the "man is responsible for things outside the home and woman for things in the home; absolute respect for the elders and obedience to authority must be rendered; the love of parents is absolutely unconditional."[156]

An interesting finding from the research is that non-Christian parents "tended to be more positive toward the value of the family and the authority of the elders than Christian parents," while "Christian parents tended to be more understanding and tolerant of the younger generation."[157] The study shows the younger generation is more westernized and that Christians are more open to change (H. C. Peng, "Generation Gap," *Campus*, 1982, 24-5:2-4).[158]

The changing Chinese culture, even in Taiwan, may help us better understand the conflicts between ABC and OBC Chinese Christians in America.[159] The H. C. Peng study points to a hopeful sign that Christian parents are more open to change. The Chinese church has great potential to help the ABC and OBC bridge the generation gap.

Differences between OBC and ABC

Samuel Ling sees the following differences between OBC and ABC.

---

[152] Tan, in Cecilia Yau, ed., 7-8.
[153] Tan, in Cecilia Yau, ed., 7-8.
[154] Tan, in Cecilia Yau, ed., 9-10.
[155] Tan, in Cecilia Yau, ed., 10.
[156] Tan, in Cecilia Yau, ed., 10.
[157] Tan, in Cecilia Yau, ed., 10.
[158] Tan, in Cecilia Yau, ed., 10.
[159] Tan, in Cecilia Yau, ed., 10.

1. The individual vs. the group. Western culture values autonomous individuals while Chinese culture values the cohesiveness of the family or clan.[160]
2. Theory vs. relationship. The American way of facing a problem or need is to make a study to find the best way to solve it. The Chinese way is to find a solution without offending anyone.[161]
3. Differences vs. equality. The American Christian looks at the pastor as a friend, while Chinese Christians look at the pastor as the leader.[162] The Chinese pastor expects the younger generation to show respect and loyalty to him. Ling writes of the Chinese pastor's thinking, "In his or her mind, loyalty to the pastor and faithfulness to the ministry of the church are one and the same thing."[163]
4. Love vs. respect. The American way of showing affection and love is to show it outwardly with a hug or kiss. For the Chinese, Ling writes, "Rules and regulations are ways the Chinese community preserves harmony, order, and respect. Think of 'respect' as the Chinese equivalent of 'love.'"[164]
5. Self-confidence vs. humility. While Americans talk about their strength and accomplishments, the Chinese would hide their accomplishments and emphasize their weaknesses in public.[165] Ling notes this has a detrimental effect on the success of Chinese in the corporate world. He observes, "The Chinese race has suffered from a corporate identity crisis for the past one hundred fifty years. Lack of confidence and security has plagued our people as a whole."[166]
6. Organism vs. organization. The ABCs are used to organizational structure, while the traditional Chinese is basically uncomfortable with structure. The Western mindset is oriented to things logical, cognitive, and intellectual while the Chinese mindset is oriented to either the mystical/natural, or to the pragmatic/social.[167] Ling writes, "Translated into everyday life, this means that the traditional Chinese mind is basically uncomfortable with organization, red-tape, paper-work, official and formal lines of authority, formal membership in an organization, and business meetings."[168] The Western mind can be seen as more "left-

---

[160] Ling and Cheuk, 143.
[161] Ling and Cheuk, 146.
[162] Ling and Cheuk, 148.
[163] Ling and Cheuk, 148.
[164] Ling and Cheuk, 149.
[165] Ling and Cheuk, 151.
[166] Ling and Cheuk, 152.
[167] Ling and Cheuk, 153.
[168] Ling and Cheuk, 153.

brain" or cognitive, while the Chinese mind can be seen as more "right-brain" or aesthetic.[169]

7. Leadership: credentials vs. service record. Western societies have formalized ways of recognizing leadership through academic degree or professional license.

8. The Chinese laypeople recognize the pastor as the leader not through their degree or ordination, but through their years of consistent faithful service.[170]

9. Spiritual gifts vs. secular credentials. The Chinese also have "great *secular* expectations of their leaders in addition to the spiritual qualifications."[171] Ling observes these secular credentials can include: older age, ability to speak Chinese, family background, advanced degrees from universities or seminaries, marriage and children, house, and a middle-class status.[172] This is different from Westerners where leadership qualification is through academic training and professional experience.[173]

10. Lubrication and preservation: implicit or explicit. Ling mentions the importance of the wedding ceremony to the Chinese. He writes, "It is a communal affair. The pastor represents God's blessing upon the bride and groom, and also God's blessing upon the two families."[174] Ling suggests the Americanized person should understand "the tremendous importance of these rituals of value affirmation for the Chinese family and community."[175]

11. Conflict management: confrontation vs. conciliation. For Americans, direct confrontation is normal and expected; but for Chinese, this would be "face destroying" and can even tear apart a community.[176] For Chinese, it is more acceptable to deal with conflict through "indirect conciliation."[177] For example, a person at church would first talk to another responsible layperson about an issue he is concerned with. The responsible layperson would then convey this concern to the pastor or the official board.[178]

---

[169] Ling and Cheuk, 153.
[170] Ling and Cheuk, 155.
[171] Ling and Cheuk, 156.
[172] Ling and Cheuk, 156.
[173] Ling and Cheuk, 156.
[174] Ling and Cheuk, 158.
[175] Ling and Cheuk, 158.
[176] Ling and Cheuk, 159.
[177] Ling and Cheuk, 159.
[178] Ling and Cheuk, 159.

Bicultural Chinese

Gail Law sees that the OBC and ABC categories, which are based on the place of birth "may be convenient and helpful as descriptive categories," though "they are misleading if used to make diagnostic statements—for example, as the root cause of tension between the OBCs and ABCs."[179]

Law explains that Chinese churches often see themselves through "The Static-Dichotomous-Discontinuous Model" (SDD Model).[180] He proposes "The Dynamic-Bicultural-Continuum Model" (DBC Model).[181] The DBC Model shows two opposite categories: the "culturally Chinese" who embraces Chinese values only and the "culturally American" who embraces American (or Western) values only. In between these two categories are the "bicultural Chinese with varying degrees of mixing between their 'Chinese-ness' and 'American-ness.'" [182]

Law attributes the cause of ABCs leaving the Chinese churches to the bicultural gap.[183] Law believes the way to resolve this is for one or both groups to move towards the other group. He writes, "There are at least three possible ways to bridge this gap: to expand the bicultural-ness of the Chinese church further into the area of "American-ness," to expand the bicultural-ness of the ABCs further into the area of "Chinese-ness," or to do both."[184]

Law sees a healthy bicultural church relies on the guidance of the Holy Spirit following the teachings of the scriptures, not merely selectively choosing desirable elements from the two cultures.[185] Law believes this will transform the Chinese community and enrich the Christian experience in North America. He writes, "In this way the expression of the Christian faith in a bi-cultural ethnic Chinese church would be fuller than that of a monocultural one."[186]

Hybridization of Chinese Culture

The ethnic identity of Chinese in the SFBA will change with each succeeding generation. The first generation would retain the most memory of the old culture and the second and later generations may not observe all the traditions of their parents and lose the culture and language of their parents. [187]

In the Chinese community of the Silicon Valley, one can see mixtures of elements from different regional cultures. Bernard Wong observes, "In Santa

---

[179] Law, in Cecilia Yau, ed., 132.
[180] Law, in Cecilia Yau, ed., 132.
[181] Law, in Cecilia Yau, ed., 134.
[182] Law, in Cecilia Yau, ed., 134.
[183] Law, in Cecilia Yau, ed., 137.
[184] Law, in Cecilia Yau, ed., 138.
[185] Law, in Cecilia Yau, ed., 138.
[186] Law, in Cecilia Yau, ed., 138.
[187] Bernard P. Wong, 197.

Clara's Chinese Rice Stix Restaurant, one sees the hybridization of Chinese dim sum items that include Chinese-style Portuguese egg tarts, Chinese-style Portuguese chicken, tapioca pearl teas, Northern Chinese dumplings, small (short) grain porridge, and sticky rice pork dumplings. These dishes are hybrids from several regional cuisines or national traditions."[188]

There may be a hybridization of lifestyle and cultural values in the Chinese immigrant. For example, a Chinese immigrant may like American democracy but prefer Chinese culture. He may like American houses, universities, and the physical environments; but also prefer the Chinese way of social interaction, which he feels is more humane and personal.[189]

Hybridity

Marwan M. Kraidy in *Hybridity, or the Cultural Logic of Globalization,* notes that hybridity "is one of the emblematic notions of our era. It captures the spirit of the times with its obligatory celebration of cultural difference and fusion, and it resonates with the globalization mantra of unfettered economic exchanges and the supposedly inevitable transformation of all cultures."[190] Kraidy uses the term "hybridity" to refer mostly to culture, but the word can also relate to the "interconnected realms of race, language, and ethnicity."[191]

Hybridity involves the fusion of two distinct cultures that can occur across national borders or cultural boundaries.[192] Kraidy believes that communication through international media programs or through the migration of people is key to hybridity.[193] The motivation of the international media programs can be commercial interests or "geostrategic considerations."[194] The motivation of migration can be caused by the push/pull factors of poverty and repression and the hope for upward mobility.[195]

Kraidy proposes "critical transculturalism" as a new hybridity model. He contrasts it with cultural imperialism and cultural pluralism. He writes, "whereas cultural imperialism focuses on the production and distribution stages of the media communication process, and cultural pluralism emphasizes message/text and reception, critical transculturalism takes a more integrative approach that considers the active links between production, text, and reception in the moment of cultural reproduction."[196]

---

[188] Bernard P. Wong, 199.
[189] Bernard P. Wong, 199.
[190] Marwan M. Kraidy, *Hybridity, or the Cultural Logic of Globalization,* (Philadelphia, PA: Temple University, 2005), 1.
[191] Kraidy, 1.
[192] Kraidy, 5.
[193] Kraidy, 5.
[194] Kraidy, 5.
[195] Kraidy, 5.
[196] Kraidy, 149-150.

Critical transculturalism does not see culture as stable and autonomous units. It sees cultures as "mutually constitutive, a perspective advanced in terms of 'glocalization' (Kraidy, 2003b; Robertson, 1994), 'interpenetrated globalization' (Braman, 1996), or 'distant proximities' (Rosenau, 2003)."[197] Kraidy also sees socioeconomic structures can enable, hinder, or even cripple the formation of hybridity. He points to the example from the 2000 U.S. Census when a multiracial option encouraged people to see themselves in a hybrid identity.[198]

Globalization and Identity Formation

The ethnic identity of the Chinese in the Silicon Valley is influenced by their home country, the home region where they are from, and the place in America where they lived. Many of the Chinese immigrants in the Silicon Valley work in multinational corporations and some are working temporarily in Asia. As these travel between continents and national borders, they establish many sets of networks in their life. They may have family and friends in the Silicon Valley while their relatives are in home countries like Taiwan, Hong Kong, mainland China, and Singapore.[199]

The Silicon Valley Chinese community consists of high-tech workers who are participating fully in the global economy. These Chinese immigrants can enjoy the best of both Chinese and American cultures in the Silicon Valley with its informal social networks and flexible modes of earning a living. They can establish roots in America and at the same time live with Chinese culture as well as the regional culture. Bernard Wong writes, "It is perhaps the latest experiment in a transnational existence to be found in modern multicultural America."[200]

Summary

This study shows the Chinese came to the United States in large numbers starting from the 1850s. Despite periodic restrictions, they have become a sizable and successful community in the US today. The Protestant work among the Chinese also began in California from the 1850s. Today, Chinese churches are growing due to Chinese immigrations over the years. In 2008, in the San Francisco Bay area alone, researchers counted 194 Chinese churches and

---

[197] Kraidy, 154.
[198] Kraidy, 158.
[199] Bernard P. Wong, 235.
[200] Bernard P. Wong, 241.

attendance over 30,000.[201] There were 37 new Chinese churches started from 1996 to 2008.[202] We see in the Chinese diaspora the hardworking nature, Chinese-oriented unity and fellowship, and harmony. The Chinese culture includes the avoidance of confrontation, emphasis on relationship, high-context, and honor and shame. There is sub-cultural difference between mainland Chinese, Taiwan Chinese, Hong Kong Chinese, and other Southeast Asian Chinese. Among these ethnic groups are the OBC, ARC, and ABC, each having different levels of acculturation to the American society. Chinese immigrants in the SFBA also experience hybridization of lifestyle and cultural values, as they establish roots in America and at the same time live with Chinese culture as well as the regional culture.

---

[201] Chuck and Tseng, eds., 5.
[202] Chuck and Tseng, eds., 4-5.

CHAPTER 3
DIASPORA MISSIOLOGY: HISTORY, THEOLOGY, AND CURRENT ISSUES

Introduction

The importance of ministering to minorities and immigrants is clearly in the heart of God, starting from the Old Testament. Arthur F. Glasser writes, "The extended emphasis in the Old Testament on the 'stranger within the gates' means that the church-in-mission today must give priority to the needs of all minority and immigrant people, an issue particularly important today with regard to the millions of displaced and refugee people we find all over the globe."[203] J. D. Payne also points to the theme of migration in human history, "The history of humanity is a history of migration. Ever since the exodus from Eden (Gen. 3:23-24), men and women have been on the move."[204]

The European expansion in the 1500s began a new era in migration history. Large numbers of people came to the United States from Europe in the nineteenth and twentieth centuries. Migration became a global phenomenon in the latter part of the twentieth and early twenty-first century, through faster and safer forms of transportation, new political structures, and advances in telecommunications.[205]

Payne believes in continuing to send missionaries throughout the world yet also recognizes the Great Commission opportunity in Western nations. He sees a problem when Christians are willing to send people overseas and ignore the unreached people who live in their own neighborhoods. He writes, "something is missiologically malignant when we are willing to send people across the oceans, risking life and limb and spending enormous amounts of money; but we are not willing to walk next door and minister to the strangers living there."[206]

---

[203] Arthur F. Glasser, *Announcing the Kingdom: The Story of God's Mission in the Bible,* (Grand Rapids, MI: Baker Academic, 2003), 87.
[204] J. D. Payne, *Strangers Next Door: Immigration, Migration and Mission,* (Downers Grove, IL: IVP, 2012), 29.
[205] Payne, 29.
[206] Payne, 33.

There is great potential to reach the world's unreached and least reached people through local missions. Payne writes, "The Lord of the harvest has been moving some of the world's unreached and least reached people to countries where governmental opposition will not interfere with missionary labors and where obtaining a visa and the costs of travel are not issues."[207] A new type of mission strategy can be seen through God's providential moving of people around the world.

Wan defines "diaspora missions" as "the Christian's participation in God's redemptive mission to evangelize their kinsmen on the move and through them to natives in their homeland and beyond."[208]

Wan sees the following advantages in diaspora missions:[209]

1. It is not programmatic, not entrepreneur, not outcome-based.
2. It has a strong emphasis on relational dimensions between person Being (the triune God) and beings (of humanity and angelic reality).
3. It recognizes the dimension of spiritual warfare.
4. It involves vertical dimensions, e.g. "relational accountability."
5. It is "glocal" missions in the globalized context.
6. It is non-spatial, "borderless," no boundary to worry, and transnational.
7. It is a different approach: integrated ministry.
8. It is about learning a new demographic reality of the 21st century and strategizing accordingly with good stewardship.

Diaspora missions involves at the micro level: love, compassion, Christian hospitality. At the macro level, it involves partnership and networking. It is a holistic Christianity with strong integration of evangelism with Christian compassion and charity. It is "Great commission" plus "Great commandment."[210] Wan sees that diaspora missions include "ministering to and through and beyond the diaspora, relational accountability, strategic stewardship, and partnership."[211]

Historical Development of Diaspora Missiology

The following traces diachronically the conferences, organizations, papers, and books which contributed to the development of diaspora missiology.

---

[207] Payne, 33.
[208] Payne, 145.
[209] Wan, *Diaspora Missiology: Theory, Methodology, and Practice*, 148.
[210] Wan, *Diaspora Missiology: Theory, Methodology, and Practice*, 149.
[211] Wan, *Diaspora Missiology: Theory, Methodology, and Practice*, 149.

The Lausanne Movement played an important role in the development of diaspora missiology. After ICCOWE in Lausanne in 1974, the Chinese participants founded the Chinese Coordinating Committee for World Evangelization in 1976 in Hong Kong. S. Hun Kim and Wonsuk Ma see this mission organization as the first concrete action in diaspora mission.[212] The Lausanne Diaspora Movement was organized after Lausanne II in Manila (1989) and the first international Diaspora Leadership Consultation was held in Edmonton, Alberta, Canada in 1998.[213]

In June 2002, The American Society of Missiology (AMS) annual meeting chose the theme "Migration Challenge and Avenue for Christian Mission." The proceedings were published in *Missiology* XXXI (January 2003). The papers included "Mission among the Chinese diaspora: A case study of migration and mission" by Enoch Wan, "Offering Hospitality to Strangers" by Christine Pohl, "The Mission of Migrant Churches in Europe" by Jan Jongenee, and "Responding to the Challenge of Migration: Churches (WCC)" by Jean Stromberg. Samuel Escobar and Daniel Rodriguez also contributed papers on the Hispanic diaspora in the United Sates and Spain.[214]

The Seoul Consultation in Seoul, Korea from April 12-15, 2004, was sponsored by Filipino International Network (FIN).[215] As the result of the Seoul Consultation, FIN published a volume on Filipino diaspora.[216] This volume covered the study of diaspora missiology in five parts: historical demography, biblical theology, missiological methodology, global strategy (evangelism and discipleship), and personal stories of Filipino "Kingdom workers."[217] As the chief editor of this volume, Enoch Wan integrated historic-demographic facts with biblical-theological data.[218]

The 2004 Lausanne Forum held in Pattaya, Thailand had a "diaspora" issue group for the first time in LCWE (Lausanne Congress of World Evangelization). This issue group produced the Lausanne Occasional Paper (LOP No. 55) "The New People Next Door," which is the first-ever Lausanne paper on diaspora.[219] This paper included discussion on biblical and theological bases for diaspora ministry and contained case studies on Chinese, Filipino, South Asian, Persian, and international students.[220] Wan sees the publication of LOP No. 55 as

---

[212] S. Hun Kim and Wonsuk Ma, *Korean Diaspora and Christian Mission,* (Eugene, OR: Wipf and Stock Publishers, 2011), 1.

[213] Kim and Ma, 1.

[214] Enoch Wan, *Diaspora Missiology: Theory, Methodology, and Practice,* 2nd ed. (Portland, OR: Institute of Diaspora Studies, 2014), 136.

[215] Wan, *Diaspora Missiology*, 2nd ed., 136.

[216] Kim and Ma, 1, and Wan, *Diaspora Missiology,* 2nd ed., 136.

[217] Wan, *Diaspora Missiology,* 2nd ed., 136-137.

[218] Wan, *Diaspora Missiology,* 2nd ed., 137.

[219] Wan, *Diaspora Missiology,* 2nd ed., 137.

[220] Wan, *Diaspora Missiology,* 2nd ed., 137.

significant because "it helped to place 'diaspora missiology' on the global agenda of the Church."[221]

The Filipino Diaspora Missions Consultation was held April 12-15, 2004 at the Torch Trinity Graduate School of Theology in Seoul, Republic of South Korea.[222]

During January 4-6, 2006, the Filipino Theological Educator's Consultation at the Philippine Baptist Theological Seminary, Baguio City, Philippines, was attended by dozens of missiologists and theological educators from the USA, Canada, Korea, and the Philippines. These came together "to strategize ways and means to promote both formal and informal education in diaspora missiology for pastors, missionaries, and Filipino Kingdom workers around the world."[223]

Within the period November 15-18, 2006, LCWE endorsed the first Global Diaspora Missiology Consultation, sponsored by FIN (Filipino International Network), which was held at Taylor University College and Seminary (Edmonton, Alberta, Canada). In the meeting, case studies were presented by ministry practitioners on major diaspora groups such as Chinese, Jewish, Filipino, South Asian, Kenyan, Korean, Vietnamese, Tibetan, Nepalese, and Hispanic.[224]

In the Spring 2007 EMS *Occasional Bulletin*, Enoch Wan wrote an article "Diaspora Missiology," which "defines diaspora missiology and delineates its contents, distinctiveness, and methodology."[225] *Global Missiology*, a multi-lingual free online journal, also focused on diaspora missiology in its July 2007 issue.[226]

Enoch Wan describes his early journey in diaspora studies: [227]

Due to my interest in diaspora studies, my years of missionary service in Philippines and Australia provided me opportunities to study various diaspora groups (with a focus on Chinese) in two continents. My teaching and pastoral ministries careers in Canada, Hong Kong, and the United States allowed me to continue this pursuit. I started the first "Center of Chinese Study" in North America at Canadian Theological Seminary and served as the director from 1982 to 1988. In 1988, it was expanded to included five diaspora groups at the founding of the Centre of Intercultural Studies (CIS). In 1994 CIS organized the first Intercultural Ministries National Conference

---

[221] Wan, *Diaspora Missiology*, 2nd ed., 137.
[222] Wan, *Diaspora Missiology*, 2nd ed., 137.
[223] Wan, *Diaspora Missiology*, 2nd ed., 137.
[224] Wan, *Diaspora Missiology*, 2nd ed., 137.
[225] Wan, *Diaspora Missiology*, 2nd ed., 141.
[226] Wan, *Diaspora Missiology*, 2nd ed., 141.
[227] Enoch Wan, "Diaspora Missiology and Beyond: Paths Taken and Ways Forward," Michael Pocock and Enoch Wan, eds., *Diaspora Missions: Reflections on Reaching the Scattered Peoples of the World,* (Pasadena, CA: William Carey Library, 2015), 218.

of Canada and published the compendium volume *Missions within Reach: Intercultural Ministries in Canada* --- a prototype of diaspora missiology.

In 2009, the Lausanne Diaspora Leadership Team (LDLT) was formed.[228] For two years, the Korean Diaspora Forum (KDF) and the Korean Diaspora Missions Network (KODIMNET) contributed research works to produce a volume in 2011 about Korean diaspora mission in the world.[229] In 2009 in Manila, the Lausanne Diaspora Leadership Team developed a theological foundation for diaspora missiology.[230] In 2007, Western Seminary (Portland, Oregon) launched The Institute for Diaspora Studies (IDS-USA), which is "a joint effort of researchers of diaspora missiology, trainers, and practitioners seeking to practice diaspora missions in the 21st century."[231] IDS-Asia, a branch of IDS, was launched on April 1, 2007, at Alliance Graduate School of Theology in Manila, Philippines.[232]

In November 2009 in Seoul, the Lausanne Diaspora Educators Consultation formulated the "Seoul Declaration on Diaspora Missiology."[233] A working committee was formed to produce the booklet *Scattered to Gather: Embracing the Global Trend of Diaspora*, which was distributed at the Lausanne Cape Town 2010 conference.[234] In April 2010, a diaspora conference was held in Oxford to explore specifically European cases.[235]

On May 25, 2010, at the International Forum for Migrant Mission (IFMM) in Seoul, Korea, Enoch Wan gave a presentation on "Diaspora Missiology in Action: A Case Study of Chinese Diaspora Missions & CCCOWE," where he challenged the Korean participants to form a global network in diaspora mission.[236]

In the 2010 Third Lausanne Congress in Cape Town, South Africa, "the issue of diaspora and its missiology was one of the predominant features of the whole programme and acclaimed as a paradigm for world evangelization."[237] In the middle of the Congress, on October 20, 2010, the [Lausanne] Global Diaspora Network Advisory Board was formed to take the place of the Lausanne Diaspora Leadership Team, with Sadiri Joy Tira serving as the chairperson for the Global Diaspora Network (GDN).[238] Tira also serves as the Senior Associate for Diasporas.[239]

---

[228] Kim and Ma, 2.
[229] Kim and Ma, 1.
[230] Kim and Ma, 2.
[231] Institute of Dispoara Studies (IDS), <http://www.westernseminary.edu/centers/institute-of-diaspora-studies> (12/25/2015).
[232] Wan, *Diaspora Missiology*, 2nd ed., 145.
[233] Kim and Ma, 2.
[234] Wan, *Diaspora Missiology*, 2nd ed.,138.
[235] Kim and Ma, 2.
[236] Wan, *Diaspora Missiology*, 2nd ed.,139-140.
[237] Kim and Ma, 2.
[238] Kim and Ma, 2, and Wan, *Diaspora Missiology*, 2nd ed.,138.
[239] Wan, *Diaspora Missiology*, 2nd ed., 138.

The GDN headquarters/secretariat office was established in Manila in 2011.[240] In June 2011, at the Lausanne Leadership Biennial Meeting in Boston, Massachusetts, the 2015 World Diaspora Forum was announced to be held in the Philippines March 24-28, 2015, sponsored by the Lausanne Committee.[241]

August 11-14, 2011, GDN hosted "The Far East Asia Educators Forum" in Manila. The purpose was to develop "courses and curriculum to train workers and researchers to advance the cause of diaspora mission and ministry."[242]

During February 14-17, 2012, the 8th Korean Diaspora Forum (KDF) met in Johannesburg, South Africa. The theme was "Beyond Barrier, Beyond Generations." KDF was started in 2004 in Baltimore, USA. KDF has met annually since 2005: Beijing-2006, Tokyo-2007, Kuala Lumpur-2008, Shanghai-2009, Seol-Ak Mountain-2010, Los Angeles 2011.[243]

In March 2012, The Pew Research Center's Forum on Religion & Public Life published *Faith on the Move* on the religions of international immigrants. *Faith on the Move* is "a new study by the Pew Research Center's Forum on Religion & Public Life, [which] focuses on the religious affiliation of international migrants, examining patterns of migration among seven major groups: Christians, Muslims, Hindus, Buddhists, Jews, adherents of other religions and the religiously unaffiliated." [244] In December 2012, The Pew Research Center published *The Global Religious Landscape: A Report on the Size and Distribution of the World's Major Religious Groups as of 2010*.[245]

The 2011 case study of Greenhills Christian Fellowship in the Philippines shows an example of diaspora mission "by and beyond" the diaspora. This study was done by Sadiri Joy Tira and Narry F. Santos ("Diaspora church planting in a multicultural city: A case study of Greenhills Christian Fellowship," in *Reflecting God's Glory Together: Diversity in Evangelical Mission*, edited by A. Scott Moreau and Beth Snodderly) and referenced in Enoch Wan's *Diaspora Missiology*, 2nd edition.[246]

In 2012, J. D. Payne wrote *Strangers Next Door: Immigration, Migration, and Mission.* Wan noted this book "presents helpful demographic data and calls for Christians to actively engage in diaspora mission by reaching out to incoming migrants and immigrants in our neighborhood."[247]

---

[240] Wan, *Diaspora Missiology*, 2nd ed., 138.
[241] Wan, *Diaspora Missiology*, 2nd ed., 138-139.
[242] Wan, *Diaspora Missiology*, 2nd ed., 139.
[243] Wan, *Diaspora Missiology*, 2nd ed., 139.
[244] *Faith on the Move*: The Religious Affiliation of International Migrants, 2012 produced by Pew Research Center, Pew Forum for Religion and Public Life, <http://www.pewforum.org/files/2012/03/Faithonthemove.pdf> (12/25/2015), 11.
[245] *The Global Religious Landscape*, 2012 produced by Pew Research Center, Pew Forum for Religion and Public Life, <http://www.pewforum.org/files/2014/01/global-religion-full.pdf> (12/25/2015)
[246] Wan, *Diaspora Missiology*, 2nd ed., 143.
[247] Wan, *Diaspora Missiology*, 2nd ed., 143.

On April 18-20, 2013, the 12th Ethnic Ministries Summit was held in Chicago. The theme was "Mission on Our Doorsteps." This coalition of Christian ministries and churches from across the USA and Canada has held annual Ethnic Ministries Summits since 2000.[248]

The theme of the Evangelical Missiological Society in 2014 was "Diaspora Missiology" and the theme of the 2014 North American Mission Leaders Conference was "Migration and Mission."[249]

There have been many dissertations completed and in progress at Western Seminary on diaspora missiology topics. The dissertations are related to diasporas such as: Jews, Filipino, Ghanaian, Hispanics in the USA, Vietnamese, Yunnanese Chinese community in Lashio, Myanmar, Korean, Japanese, and Sri Lankan. There are also many doctoral dissertations in progress on other diaspora groups.[250]

Diaspora in the Bible

The first migration in the book of Genesis occurred when Adam and Eve were banished out of the Garden of Eden (Gen. 3:23-24). Later, Cain wandered the earth after killing his brother Abel (Gen. 4:12-16). Following the flood, God scattered the peoples all over the earth from Babel (Gen.11:8-9). Abraham migrated from Mesopotamia (Gen. 12:1-9), and his descendants such as Jacob and Jacob's sons also had to migrate (Gen. 27, 31, 38).[251] Andrew F. Walls sees the first book of the Bible might as well be called "Migrations" as Genesis.[252] Exodus, the second book of the Bible, describes the migration of Israel out of Egypt and on the way to the Promise Land. In Israel's history, God's divine judgments on Israel for her sins forced Israel's migration to Assyria (2 Kgs 17:5-23) and Babylon (2 Kgs 25).[253]

Walls notes in the Bible, "If we take all the stories together, we have examples of almost every known form of migration, voluntary and involuntary."[254] We can see this in the Bible stories of fugitives, refugees, traders, invaders, prisoners of war, deportees, and returnees.[255] Walls sees the migration in biblical stories can be punitive as well as redemptive. Examples of punitive cases are when Adam is banished from Eden, when Cain is banished to

---

[248] Wan, *Diaspora Missiology,* 2nd ed., 140.

[249] Wan, *Diaspora Missiology,* 2nd ed., 140.

[250] Wan, *Diaspora Missiology,* 2nd ed., 143-144.

[251] Andrew F. Walls, "Mission and Migration: The Diaspora Factor in Christian History," in *Global Diasporas and Mission*, Chandler H. Im and Amos Yong (Eugene, OR: Wipf and Stock Publishers, 2014), 19.

[252] Walls, in Im and Yong, 19.

[253] Walls, in Im and Yong, 19.

[254] Walls, in Im and Yong, 19.

[255] Walls, in Im and Yong, 19.

wander the earth, and when the Israelites are taken captive to Assyria and Babylon.[256] Examples of redemptive cases are when Abraham is called out of Mesopotamia and he and his descendants settled in the Promised land.[257] Thus, Walls sees there are two types of migration in the biblical record – "Adamic" which involves "disaster, deprivation, and loss" and "Abrahamic" which "stands for escape to a superlatively better future."[258]

God used the scattered Jews to spread the knowledge of Himself and the Old Testament Bible throughout the Mediterranean world. Wall writes, "It is clear, for instance, that the earliest spread of the faith beyond Jewish Palestine owed much to prior Jewish migration across the Mediterranean world, as well as into Mesopotamia and beyond."[259] Through the spread of diaspora Judaism, Gentiles were attracted to the worship of God and this prepared them to be receptive to the early Christian preaching, more than the diaspora Jews.[260]

In the Book of Acts, we see how involuntary and voluntary migration contributed to the spread of the gospel. In Acts 1:8, Jesus commands His disciples to be His witnesses in Jerusalem, Judea, Samaria, and to the ends of the earth. This foreshadows the global migration of God's people to spread the good news. In Acts 2:8-9, we see there were visitors to Jerusalem from Asia, Media, Rome, and Crete. These visitors made the trip to Jerusalem for Pentecost and many would later return to their homelands to spread the gospel after believing in Christ.

In the selection of the Seven who were to serve in the daily distribution of food in Acts 6:1-6, we see diaspora people mentioned in the Jerusalem church, such as Nicolas from Antioch, who was a convert to Judaism.

In Acts 8:1, the church in Jerusalem was scattered by a great persecution after the stoning of Stephen. Acts 8 tells how these scattered disciples preached the good news wherever they went and people in Samaria believed as well as an Ethiopian eunuch. Saul was traveling to the synagogues in Damascus when he met the Lord and was baptized in Damascus (Acts 9:18).

Cornelius the centurion is a diaspora Italian who lived in Caesarea. He was saved through the preaching of Peter (Acts 10). We see here the case where a non-believer from a non-Christian ethnic group was converted when he lived in the vicinity of the Jewish Christians. Acts 11:19-21 tells how the Lord's hand was with the scattered Jewish Christians who preached the gospel to the Greeks. These new Gentile believers were in Antioch, where the first major non-Jewish Christian community was formed. The disciples were first called Christians at Antioch (Acts 11:26). The prophets and teachers in the church at Antioch were

---

[256] Walls, in Im and Yong, 20.
[257] Walls, in Im and Yong, 20.
[258] Walls, in Im and Yong, 21.
[259] Walls, in Im and Yong, 21.
[260] Walls, in Im and Yong, 21.

diaspora people such as Barnabas, Simeon called Niger, Lucius of Cyrene, and Saul.

Paul and Barnabas were sent on missionary journeys by the Antioch church in Acts 13. They first went to the gatherings of the Jews in the diaspora communities of Asia Minor and Europe. There were Jews and Gentiles who believed, in the places they visited such as Iconium, Lystra, and Derbe (Acts 14).

In Acts 18:1-11, Paul met Aquila and Priscilla in Corinth, who were Jewish Christian believers. Having been expelled from Rome by Claudius, they became ministry partners with Paul. In Acts 18:24-28, we meet another diaspora Jew named Apollos, who is born in Alexandria, and moved to Ephesus. He became a bold and great preacher in the early church after having been instructed by Priscilla and Aquila more fully about Christ.

Enoch Wan points to Priscilla and Aquila as a case study of diaspora missions.[261] He writes, "The characteristics of Priscilla and Aquila as a diaspora couple are listed as follows:[262]

1. Ready to be mobile for the sake of the gospel while on the move: in Pontus, Rome, Corinth, Ephesus, and Rome.
2. Adaptable to circumstances and willing to play multiple roles for the gospel, i.e., tent-making, hosting missionary Paul, coaching Apollos, etc.
3. Faithful and sacrificial service in life-threatening circumstances.

These may be the characteristics of "full-time" ministry workers today, since most people would not move for missionary purposes, unless they were involved in vocational ministry. However, these may be the characteristics of modern-day missionaries, who need to move continuously to minister to the diaspora people who are moving to different places around the world.

Jared Looney tells the story of Bob who originally went to a Muslim country in West Africa to work in a village. Due to a life-threatening illness, he returned to the United States. He was disappointed about this closed door. However, he learned of an opportunity to conduct a missiological project in New York City and was told there were opportunities to work with African immigrants in New York. Bob started talking to the West African immigrants in New York and they were amazed that he could speak their language. Bob used what he learned as a missionary to minister to the African immigrants in New York, such as using oral storytelling to share Bible stories. He became the spiritual leader among the West Africans. Looney writes, "Even many who hold to their Muslim faith identify him essentially as 'their Christian pastor.'"[263]

---

[261] Wan, *Diaspora Missiology*, 2nd ed., 165.
[262] Wan, *Diaspora Missiology*, 2nd ed., 165.
[263] Jared Looney, *Crossroads of the Nations: Diaspora, Globalization, and Evangelism*, (Portland, OR: Urban Loft Publishers, 2015), 234-236.

Through the stories in the Bible, especially with regard to the disciples and missionaries of the New Testament, we can see that migration is part of God's plan to spread the gospel and build up His church on earth.

Diaspora in Christian History

Enoch Wan lists Christian mission history as "The Apostolic Age," the first 500 years, "The Dark Ages," 500-1215 A.D., "The Medieval World" and "Age of Discovery, Reformation and Renaissance," 1215-1650 A.D., "Protestant Precursors to Missions," 1650-1792 A.D., and "The Great Century and beyond," 1792-1910.[264]

"The Apostolic Age" begins from the ascension of Jesus Christ in Acts 1. The disciples grew from 120 to thousands in the beginning of the Books of Acts. The disciples in Jerusalem, except the apostles, were scattered after Acts 8 to the surrounding areas such as Samaria and other regions. In Acts 11:19-21, these scattered Jewish Christians preached to Jews and Greeks, resulting in a church being established in Antioch. Those who believed during Pentecost went back to spread the gospel in their own distant diaspora locations. The missionary journeys of Paul and Barnabas spread the gospel and planted churches in Asia Minor and southern Europe, facilitated by routes established by the Pax Romana in the Roman Empire.[265] The method of missions during this time is through the teaching and preaching of the apostles and the formation of house-churches in the homes of Christians.[266]

In the first 500 years of Christian history, the gospel spread to the Orient (including India), the West (Europe and the British Isles), and to the south in Egypt and North Africa.[267] After Christianity was adopted by the Roman Empire, it spread to diaspora people groups in the Roman Empire through the help of local Christians and government leaders, commercial contacts and marriages.[268] Andrew Walls notes, "The history of Christianity within the Roman Empire clearly shows the importance of migrant communities who retained ties to their home locality, while traveling from one part of the empire to another, for trade, or work, or some other reason."[269]

One reason for diaspora migration is persecution, such as the example of Dionysius, Bishop of Alexandria, who was exiled in the middle of the third

---

[264] Wan, *Diaspora Missiology*, 2nd ed., 166-170.
[265] Wan, *Diaspora Missiology*, 2nd ed., 166.
[266] Wan, *Diaspora Missiology*, 2nd ed., 166.
[267] Wan, *Diaspora Missiology*, 2nd ed., 167.
[268] Wan, *Diaspora Missiology*, 2nd ed., 167.
[269] Andrew F. Walls, "Mission and Migration: The Diaspora Factor in Christian History", in *Global Diasporas and Mission*, Chandler Im and Amos Yong, eds. (Eugene, OR: Wipf and Stock Publishers), 21.

century to a remote oasis. While in exile, Dionysius evangelized and pastored the local people in this rural area.[270] Walls sees this as an example of the strengthening of the bond between rural and urban churches since Dionysius was from a major metropolitan church and he preached to the rural peasants using their language and accepted their hospitality during his exile.[271]

Walls points to the tensions between different congregations who want to retain their local traditions and the church officials who want to unify the traditions of the church. For example, the bishop of Rome, Victor, wanted Ephesian and other Asian churches to use the "Western" date for celebrating Easter.[272] We see how in the early church there are already conflicts over local traditions. This early Christian history example is instructive for us as we seek to contextualize and empower local churches to practice Christianity in their own culture.

A second century letter may suggest the Christian community in the Rhone Valley was formed through migration. A letter from the churches of Lyon and Vienne in the Rhone Valley was written in Greek, the names of the Christians mentioned in the letter were Greek, and it was addressed to "the brethren in Asia and Phrygia."[273] Walls thinks it "would appear that the group belonged to an Asian and Phrygian migration to the area."[274]

The establishment of Wulfila's Christian Goths in the fourth century is an example of how forced migration of Christian slaves led to a new Christian nation. In the third century, a raid by Eastern Goths took people of Pontus who were Christians as slaves to Gothic lands on the Black Sea coast. As captives and exiles, the Pontic church influenced the Gothic community. In the following century, a probably mixed-race Wulfia grew up speaking the Gothic language and became a great evangelist and Bible translator. He led the Gothic church and later the Gothic migration across the frontier to form a new Christian nation.[275]

Another migration story is that of Patrick of Ireland. As a young man, he was captured in a raid and brought to Ireland from Britain. In Ireland, Patrick became a fervent Christian and through dreams, visions, and acts of power he escaped and returned to Britain. However, dreams, visions, and acts of power brought him back to Ireland as its leading evangelist.[276] In today's language, we can say a 1.5 generation (those who immigrated at a young age) diaspora Christian became the leading evangelist in the foreign country where he grew up as a young man. We see a case where God used Patrick not in his own native

---

[270] Walls, in Im and Yong, 23.
[271] Walls, in Im and Yong, 23.
[272] Walls, in Im and Yong, 23-24.
[273] Walls, in Im and Yong, 24.
[274] Walls, in Im and Yong, 24.
[275] Walls, in Im and Yong, 24.
[276] Walls, in Im and Yong, 25.

country but in the foreign country where he lived. Thus, we see that diaspora people can be called by God back to their home country or stay in their adopted country to spread the gospel.

In another case of the invasion of Roman territory, the Persians took large numbers of Christian captives, including the Bishop of Antioch. These Christians never returned home but established an effective church as they worked in the new imperial building development. Soon, most of the people in the church no longer had Greek names but had Syriac and Iranian names. Walls observes, "This migrant church had crossed the cultural frontier and even affected its overlords."[277]

In another case of the migration of Christian captive slaves, the Hun people took Syriac-speaking Christians as slaves from the Persian Empire. These Christians eventually lead the whole Bactrian Hun community to become Christians. The new Bactrian Hun Christian community even applied to the Persian Zoroastrian emperor for a bishop to lead and teach them.[278]

During "The Dark Ages," 500-1215 A.D., Christianity spread to Russia, Moravia, Eastern Europe, Great Britain, continental Europe, and Scandinavia. The Nestorians, despite their heretical doctrines, brought the gospel to China and Asia. During this time, the Christian faith was challenged by the schism of the Eastern church and the rise of Islam. After the Muslim conquest of North Africa, many nominal Christians there converted to Islam due to social, political, military, and religious pressures. The Crusades were intended by Western Christians to reclaim the Holy Land from Islamic control and to bring the Eastern church back to fellowship with the Western church. However, the violent crusades damaged Western Christian's relationship with the Islamic world, Jews, and the Eastern Christians. Despite the low morality and violence of the crusades, the church continued to grow during this time.[279]

Walls points to trading diaspora Christian's contribution in the spread of the Christian faith. Trading diaspora brought Christian families from the church of the East to India and Sri Lanka and possibly to South East Asia through trade routes that ran through South Arabia and Yemen. These trading diaspora Christians brought an already organized church with them as they worked.[280]

Another kind of migration is the missionary migration during this period.[281] This is more prevalent in the Eastern church than in the Western church. These missionary migrants were "corps of devoted people able and willing to travel immense distances, and live under the harshest conditions" to spread the gospel.[282] By the end of the eighth and the beginning of the ninth centuries,

---

[277] Walls, in Im and Yong, 25.
[278] Walls, in Im and Yong, 25-26.
[279] Wan, *Diaspora Missiology*, 2nd ed., 167.
[280] Walls, in Im and Yong, 26.
[281] Walls, in Im and Yong, 26.
[282] Walls, in Im and Yong, 26.

there were organized churches along the Silk Road of Central Asia and in the former Persian Empire.[283]

While migration has contributed to the spread of Christianity, it has also contributed to the near destruction of the church in the East. In the case of the Mongols who conquered Eastern Europe and Asia, Walls notes, "It suffices to say that the eventual decision of the principal body of the Mongols to embrace Islam remains a turning point in the history of religion, and in the decline of the older Asian Christianity."[284]

During "The Medieval World" and "Age of Discovery, Reformation and Renaissance" period, 1215-1650 A.D., the Western church was at the height of its religious and political power while the Eastern church was surviving through a fortress mentality.[285] During this period, Christianity still existed in India and Ethiopia but the Nestorian work in China was suppressed.[286] Some Franciscan missionaries went to China during this period and 100,000 Chinese people were converted through the efforts of John of Monte Corvino. However, in 1369 these Latin missionaries were expelled from Peking, thus ending another missionary effort to China.[287] During this period the Protestant movement was born, and the Catholic Church responded with a counter-reformation. The Jesuits became a new Catholic missionary order at this time.[288] The Protestant reformers such as Luther, Zwingli, Calvin, and Knox held a faulty "territorialism" mentality about the local church and thought the Great Commission had been fulfilled by the Apostles and that Christ would return in their generation, therefore, they should focus on establishing the Reformation instead of missionary efforts.[289]

By 1500, European Christendom was expanding and the great European migration began.[290] The people who migrated from Europe were diverse. Walls notes these migrants included "adventurers and destitute or unwanted people, religious and political refugees, younger sons frustrated by European inheritance laws, discharged soldiers, convicted felons, and stable people looking for a better life or a fairer society than Europe afforded."[291]

These Europeans picked the Americas as the most favored destination while smaller numbers went to other parts of the world.[292] One of the purposes of the European migration was to propagate the Christian faith to the indigenous people in the Americas. For example, the Spanish American territories were

---

[283] Walls, in Im and Yong, 26.
[284] Walls, in Im and Yong, 27.
[285] Walls, in Im and Yong, 168.
[286] Walls, in Im and Yong, 168.
[287] Walls, in Im and Yong, 168.
[288] Walls, in Im and Yong, 169.
[289] Walls, in Im and Yong, 169.
[290] Walls, in Im and Yong, 28.
[291] Walls, in Im and Yong, 28.
[292] Walls, in Im and Yong, 28.

Christianized through the baptisms of the indigenous population and banning traditional worship.[293] The great European migration resulted in a huge number of people converted to Christianity in the non-Western world.[294]

During "Protestant Precursors to Missions," 1650-1792 A.D., Philip Spener started pietistic practices such as small group prayer meetings and Bible study groups.[295] The growth and spread of these groups led to the Moravian Mission and the Wesleyan Revival.[296] Three Anglican societies started outreach ministries to Native Americans in North America, while the William Carey Baptist Society was also started during this time, setting the stage for the next century of Christian missions.[297]

In "The Great Century and beyond," 1792-1910, Christianity expanded around the world and missions societies and organizations were formed in Europe and North America.[298] By the late nineteenth century, Christian missions included "evangelism, individual conversion, church planting, social transformation, and outreach through education and medicine."[299]

Walls writes, "By the end of the twentieth century, Christians in Africa, Asia, Latin America, and the Pacific were significantly outnumbering those of the old Christendom and North America combined."[300] While Christianity was still a European religion in 1500, it was becoming a non-Western religion by 2000.[301]

History of Other Diasporas

This section contains a brief history of the Vietnamese, Korean, and Syrian Indian diaspora. The history of these diaspora shows how Christianity is spread through the migrating people.

Vietnamese Diaspora History

Enoch Wan and Thanh Trung Le, in *Mobilizing Vietnamese Diaspora for the Kingdom,* wrote about the Vietnamese diaspora history. The first wave of Vietnamese refugees was from 1975-1977, after the North Vietnamese took over South Vietnam. This refugee group consists mostly of well-educated professionals and Westernized Vietnamese from urban areas who practiced

---

[293] Walls, in Im and Yong, 29.
[294] Walls, in Im and Yong, 31.
[295] Wan, *Diaspora Missiology,* 2nd ed., 169.
[296] Wan, *Diaspora Missiology,* 2nd ed., 169.
[297] Wan, *Diaspora Missiology,* 2nd ed., 169.
[298] Wan, *Diaspora Missiology,* 2nd ed., 170.
[299] Wan, *Diaspora Missiology,* 2nd ed., 170.
[300] Walls, in Im and Yong, 31.
[301] Walls, in Im and Yong, 31.

Roman Catholicism.[302] The second wave of Vietnamese refugees, known as the "boat people," came between 1978-1979. During this time hundreds of thousands of ethnic Chinese were also forced out of Vietnam.[303] There were 88,736 refugees in 1978 and 205,489 refugees in 1979.[304] Among these refugees, a significant number were the members from the H'mong tribes.[305] The third wave arrived from 1980-1986. It was estimated that half of the boat people, about 500,000 to 600,000 lost their lives while trying to escape on the sea.[306] The plan to grant UNHCR refugee status ended on March 6, 1996 and more than 110,000 had to return to Vietnam in the ten years following.[307]

The 2012-2013 directory of Vietnamese World Christian Fellowship, Inc. (VWCF) listed close to 30 denominations which have ministries/missions among the Vietnamese diaspora. According to this directory, there are 385 Vietnamese diaspora churches/mission points in the United States with 458 pastors. Totally there are 577 Vietnamese diaspora churches/mission points in Australia, Canada, Europe, France, Germany, Others, Asia, and the United States, with a total of 778 pastors in the Vietnamese diaspora churches.[308]

Korean Diaspora History

Minho Song gave an account of Korean diaspora history in "The Diaspora Experience of the Korean Church and its Implications for World Missions," in *Korean Diaspora and Christian Mission*. Before the end of the Chosun Dynasty (1858-1897), migration of Koreans was strictly prohibited and only diplomats were allowed to travel out of the country, because their population was seen as a symbol of power. However, the political turmoil and famine from natural disaster at the end of the Chosun dynasty caused some farmers to seek ways to move abroad and some escaped to China in the mid-nineteenth century. Russia started to develop the Maritime Province of Siberia in 1858 and encouraged people to move there. Thirteen farming families moved to this settlement near the Ussuri River in Russia in the winter of 1865 and over 4,500 farmers moved there in 1869.[309] Koreans were permitted to move to Manchuria starting in 1881.[310] A few Koreans arrived in Hawaii in 1901 and the number of Koreans in

---

[302] Enoch Wan and Thanh Trung Le, *Mobilizing Vietnamese Diaspora for the Kingdom*, (Portland, OR: Institute of Diaspora Studies of USA, 2014), 8.
[303] Wan and Le, 8.
[304] Wan and Le, 8.
[305] Wan and Le, 8.
[306] Wan and Le, 9.
[307] Wan and Le, 11.
[308] Wan and Le, 76.
[309] Minho Song, "The Diaspora Experience of the Korean Church and its Implications for World Missions," in S. Hun Kim and Wonsuk Ma, *Korean Diaspora and Christian Mission*, (Eugene, OR: Wipf & Stock Pub., 2011), 183.
[310] Song, in Kim and Ma, 183.

Hawaii grew to 7,226 in 1905.[311] Song writes, "During this period, around 40% of the 7,000 immigrants were Christian."[312] On July 4, 1903, Koreans immigrants founded a church at Mokulreyiah, Oahu Island, only six months after their arrival.[313] Koreans immigrated to the American mainland from Hawaii starting in 1903. During the Japanese occupation period (1910-1945), more than 500,000 Koreans were in Manchuria by the late 1930s.[314] Because of the 1950 Korean War, 6,000 women married American soldiers and moved to the United States from 1950 to 1964.[315] Around 5,000 war orphans were accepted by the United States from the Korean War.[316] Around 800,000 Koreans migrated between 1991 to 2001.[317] According to the Ministry of Foreign Affairs, in 2009 there were 6,822,606 Koreans living in 176 countries.[318]

The first Korean Christian community was formed in Mukden (Sheyang) in 1879.[319] Today, there are Korean churches everywhere, including places such as Tehran (Iran), Quito (Ecuador), Bishkek (Kyrgyzstan), Abidjan (Cǒte d'Ivoire), and Dhaka (Bangladesh).[320] In North America, there are over 3,000 Korean churches serving Korean immigrants.[321]

Syrian Indian Diaspora History

In "Caroling with the Keralites: The Negotiation of Gendered Space in an Indian Immigrant Church," from *Gatherings in Diaspora: Religious Communities and the New Immigration,* Sheba George wrote about the Syrian Indian diaspora history. Syrian Christianity in India claimed to have been started by converts of the apostle Thomas, who according to tradition was martyred in southern India in 72 A.D.[322] The Christians from Kerala, which is the state at the southernmost tip of India were called Syrian not because they have Syrian ancestry but because they follow the Syrian liturgy. Through the influence of Syrian missionaries starting in the seventh century, the Syrian church was established under the patriarch of Antioch.[323] The Orthodox Syrian Christian Church of

---

[311] Song, in Kim and Ma, 184.
[312] Song, in Kim and Ma, 184.
[313] Song, in Kim and Ma, 184.
[314] Song, in Kim and Ma, 186.
[315] Song, in Kim and Ma, 189.
[316] Song, in Kim and Ma, 189.
[317] Song, in Kim and Ma, 191.
[318] Song, in Kim and Ma, 191.
[319] Song, in Kim and Ma, 122.
[320] Song, in Kim and Ma, 122.
[321] Song, in Kim and Ma, 122.
[322] Sheba George, "Caroling with the Keralites: The Negotiation of Gendered Space in an Indian Immigrant Church," in R. Stephen Warner and Judith G. Wittner, eds., *Gatherings in Diaspora: Religious Communities and the New Immigration*, (Philadelphia: Temple University Press, 1998), 271.
[323] George, in Warner and Wittner, eds., 271.

India is one of the denominations in this tradition. Since 1912, it is no longer under the patriarch of Antioch and is led by the patriarch in Kerala.[324]

There was a wave of Kerala immigrants to the United States in the late 1960s from the immigration of Indian nurses.[325] From 1975 to 1979, 11.9 percent of the immigrant nurses were from India, while 11.2 percent were from Korea and 27.6 percent were from the Philippines.[326] The U.S. Immigration Nursing Relief Act of 1989 allowed about 16,000 nurses to immigrate.[327] The American Kerala Indian Christian community began through the immigration of Kerala Christian nurses who arrived first and later sponsored their families to join them. This is unique among Asian Indian immigrants in that the husbands are dependent on the wives for the immigration process.[328] The North American congregations of the Kerala Christians are still part of their mother church in India. The mother church in India assigns them to an American diocese and a bishop to oversee them on behalf of the patriarch in Kerala.[329]

Theology of Diaspora Missiology

The theology of diaspora missiology is the theology of missions that is applied to missions "to," "by," "through," and "with" diaspora groups.[330] Diaspora missiology seeks to address the way modern missions should be implemented with the current globalization and shifting of the center of Christianity from the north to south.[331] Diaspora missiology seeks to address theological issues, methodology, and strategy in world missions today.

Enoch Wan contrasts diaspora missiology with traditional missiology (coined by Samuel Escobar as "Managerial Missiology").[332] Wan defines "Managerial Missiology" as the "belief that missions can be approached like a business problem. With the right inputs, the thinking goes, the right outcomes can be assured. Any number of approaches have been hailed as the 'key' to world evangelization or to reaching particular groups – everything from contextualization to saturation evangelization."[333]

Wan defines "Managerial Missiology Paradigm" (MMP) as "the framework of engaging in the academic study of missiology by uncritically adopting the secular management paradigm and proposing the practice of Christian mission

---

[324] George, in Warner and Wittner, eds., 271.
[325] George, in Warner and Wittner, eds., 269.
[326] George, in Warner and Wittner, eds., 269.
[327] George, in Warner and Wittner, eds., 269.
[328] George, in Warner and Wittner, eds., 270.
[329] George, in Warner and Wittner, eds., 271-272.
[330] Wan, *Diaspora Missiology,* 2nd ed., 116.
[331] Wan, *Diaspora Missiology,* 2nd ed., 116.
[332] Wan, *Diaspora Missiology,* 2nd ed., ix, 111.
[333] Wan, *Diaspora Missiology,* 2nd ed., 112.

accordingly."[334] On the other hand, Wan defines the "Diaspora Missiology Paradigm" (DMP) as "a missiological framework for understanding and participating in God's redemptive mission among diaspora groups."[335]

Wan is critical of the marketing approach of MMP, which he sees as entrepreneurship and efficiency-oriented based on technology.[336] Wan sees its philosophy is based on instrumentalism (functionalism), which is receptor-oriented, "felt needs" approach that is filled with measurable success and outcome-based pragmatism.[337] He views MMP as "territorial," "Euro-American centric," delineates between sending and receiving, home and foreign mission, local and global, "emulating secular business management model," has a "humanistic and operational mentality," and uses "managerially statistical and strategic" methods.[338]

Wan gives an example of managerial mission practice in the "Short Cycle Planting" strategy, which seeks to shorten the time it takes to develop a mature church.[339] He strongly criticizes MMP as "an accumulative effect of a long process of wrong contextualization."[340]

Wan sees diaspora missiology as focusing on the "diaspora phenomena of the 21st century" and the "shifting landscape of 'Christendom'" which is beyond the concepts of the "melting-pot" (American) and "cultural mosaic" (Canadian).[341] It is the "Gospel from Everywhere to Everyone."[342]

Wan points out contemporary missiologists distinguish between "evangelism" and "missions" according to the "spatial, linguistic, and cultural barriers between the sharer and the recipients of the Gospel."[343] In diaspora missiology, people can reach diaspora individuals and communities anywhere and diaspora missiology is "more mobile, adaptive, and flexible including the practice of 'glocal' missions."[344]

Co-author Lei has the following feedback and questions about MMP vs. DMP:

1. How should we define missions in the traditional sense, when we send a missionary overseas? Should we also call it diaspora missions since we are sending someone to a place where they are not a native, therefore has the missionary become a diaspora?

---

[334] Wan, *Diaspora Missiology*, 2nd ed., 111.
[335] Wan, *Diaspora Missiology*, 2nd ed., 6.
[336] Wan, *Diaspora Missiology*, 2nd ed., 113.
[337] Wan, *Diaspora Missiology*, 2nd ed., 113.
[338] Wan, *Diaspora Missiology*, 2nd ed., 113.
[339] Wan, *Diaspora Missiology*, 2nd ed., 115.
[340] Wan, *Diaspora Missiology*, 2nd ed., 116.
[341] Wan, *Diaspora Missiology*, 2nd ed., 124.
[342] Wan, *Diaspora Missiology*, 2nd ed., 124.
[343] Wan, *Diaspora Missiology*, 2nd ed., 127.
[344] Wan, *Diaspora Missiology*, 2nd ed., 127.

2. Are we replacing traditional missiology with diaspora missiology altogether? If everyone can be seen as a diaspora when they are ministering in a place not where they are born or ministering to people who are born in another country or are the descendants of people from another country, then almost every missions work can be called diaspora missions.
3. Can there be elements of MMP in diaspora missiology? Can there be a marketing approach or entrepreneurship when engaging in diaspora missions? Would elements of MMP make the mission strategy no longer diaspora missiology? Of course, DMP is different from diaspora missiology. However, should diaspora missiology be constrained by DMP?
4. It seems a lot of the compassion ministries of diaspora missiology are ministering to the "felt needs" of the immigrants and the growth of the ethnic churches are heralded as signs of God's work. Could there be elements of instrumentalism, functionalism, and pragmatism in diaspora missiology?
5. Since "Managerial Missiology" has been promoted for so long, what missionary education process is needed to change mission workers to use DMP? How would this re-education process look? What may be missing or needs to be address in DMP? This calls for more case studies of DMP and further reflections.
6. Is it either MMP or DMP, or can people incorporate both paradigms in doing traditional and diaspora mission work?
7. If we see every kind of mission work as a kind of diaspora mission, what impact will that have on world evangelization work? What effects would it have on local evangelism and world mission? Would it cause missionary-minded Christians to choose the path of most convenience or the path of most sacrifice? Would DMP motivate more Christians to be involved in cross-cultural missions?

Diaspora Missions

Diaspora ministry is 1) serving the diaspora and 2) mobilizing the diaspora to serve others "in the name of Jesus Christ and for His sake."[345] Diaspora missions is seeing the movement of people across the globe as God's calling for all Christians to serve and reach their neighbors from other countries and cultures and for diaspora Christians to reach their kinsmen and beyond. It is part of fulfilling the Great Commission of Jesus Christ in Matthew 28:19-20, through the local communities.

Wan defines four types of diaspora missions:[346]

---

[345] Wan, *Diaspora Missiology*, 2nd ed., 5.
[346] Wan, *Diaspora Missiology*, 2nd ed., 6.

51

1. Missions to the diaspora: reaching the diaspora groups in forms of Evangelism or pre-evangelistic social services, then disciple them to become worshipping communities and congregations.
2. Missions through the diaspora: diaspora Christians reaching out to their kinsmen through networks of friendship and kinship in host countries, their homelands, and abroad.
3. Missions by and beyond the diaspora: motivating and mobilizing diaspora Christians for cross-cultural missions to other ethnic groups in their host countries, homelands, and abroad.
4. Missions with the diaspora: mobilizing non-diasporic Christians individually and institutionally to partner with diasporic groups and congregations.[347]

There is great potential for Chinese congregations in the SFBA to be involved in not only #2 missions through the diaspora but also #3 missions by and beyond the diaspora, and #4 missions with the diaspora. The authors believe engaging in local cross-cultural ministries will involve contextualizing diaspora missions and cross-cultural ministry training to the local Chinese diaspora and understanding the local cross-cultural ministries of Chinese diaspora churches in the SFBA.

There has been tremendous growth of Chinese Christian churches through evangelism efforts to the first generation Chinese who came to the U.S. Kim-Kong Chan sees that the "increasing diaspora Chinese population cannot be ignored, as it enjoys one of the highest conversion rates in Christian churches."[348] However, Chan notes that the "current growth in Chinese diaspora communities seems to be more of a target for mission to the diaspora and mission through the diaspora but has not reached the potential of 'mission by and beyond the diaspora.'"[349] The authors believe along with Chan that there is potential for more Chinese Christians to reach other ethnic groups as the diaspora Chinese Christian churches become more established and the Chinese Christians become more bi-culturally trained.[350] Chan also sees the need to counter "the current ethnocentric attitude commonly found among the Chinese diaspora churches" by giving them a global worldview.[351] The authors agree and see that cross-cultural ministry training is an important part of equipping Chinese churches to gain the vision and passion for serving and reaching people cross-culturally.

---

[347] Wan, *Diaspora Missiology*, 2nd ed., 6.
[348] Kim-Kong Chan, "Case Study 2: Missiological Implications of Chinese Christians in Diaspora," in Enoch Wan, *Diaspora Missiology: Theory, Methodology, and Practice*, (Portland, OR: Institute of Diaspora Studies – U.S., 2011), 194.
[349] Chan, in Wan, *Diaspora Missiology: Theory, Methodology, and Practice*, 193.
[350] Chan, in Wan, *Diaspora Missiology: Theory, Methodology, and Practice*, 194.
[351] Chan, in Wan, *Diaspora Missiology: Theory, Methodology, and Practice*, 194.

Contemporary Issues in Diaspora Missiology

Here are some of the issues in contemporary diaspora missiology:

1. Ministering to oral cultures.

    Enoch Wan and Anthony Casey see that "one of the most formidable challenges in ethnic ministry is how to minister to immigrants who cannot read and write or have extremely low levels of literacy."[352] They suggest using the "Chronological Bible Storying" method to minister to immigrants from oral cultures.[353] The author tells how his team recorded Bible stories in Nepali and transcribed in both Nepali and English. They would tell the story in English and have the Nepalese immigrants read along. Then they played the story in Nepali so people could hear it in their native language. This served to make sure the Nepali immigrants understood the Bible story fully in their own language, helped the Nepalese learn English, and hear American pronunciations.[354]

2. The issues of second-generation diaspora Christians in the ethnic churches.

    How diaspora churches can retain and grow their second-generation members is a major challenge. Co-author Lei has personally seen a Chinese church in the SFBA start a separate service just for the ABC young adults. They may be seeing the "the silent exodus"[355] of second-generation Chinese Christians who don't come back to their mother church after graduation from college. This situation is common in other diaspora churches as well.

    Karen J. Chai points to statistics about Korean Americans leaving the church – "a study of Korean Americans in the New York City area found that while up to 75 percent of the first generation attend church, only 5 percent of the second generation remain in the church after college."[356] Chai refers to Kwang Chung Kim and Shin Kim (1996) who observe that

---

[352] Enoch Wan and Anthony Casey, *Church Planting Among Immigrants in US Urban Centers: The "Where," "Why," and "How" of Diaspora Missiology in Action,* (Portland, OR: Institute of Diaspora studies – U.S.A, 2014), 28.

[353] Wan and Casey, 85.

[354] Wan and Casey, 88.

[355] Karen J. Chai, "Competing for the Second Generation: English-Language Ministry at a Korean Protestant Church," in R. Stephen Warner and Judith G. Wittner, eds., *Gatherings in Diaspora: Religious Communities and the New Immigration,* (Philadelphia: Temple University Press, 1998), 300.

[356] Chai, in Warner and Wittner, eds., 300.

most adult second-generation Korean Americans do not attend their parents' church, even when they are living in the same city.[357] Chai, writing about the case study of the "Paxton Korean Church," attributes the success of their English ministry partly to the willingness of the senior pastor to let them be more independent.[358] She notes ironically that "the language barrier that divided generations facilitated the success of PKC's English worship service in the end."[359] The language barrier provided a reason for a separate service for the second generation Korean Christian adults.[360]

In the case of the Syrian Indian Church, Sheba George also focused on the tension between the first and second generations in the immigrant church, especially with the teenage girls in the church who wanted to go caroling with the older men.[361] Sheba notes that in this diaspora congregation the "college-age and post college group is conspicuously absent."[362] She writes, "I believe that the American diocese needs to map out a long-term vision that addresses such issues as offering consistent English-language services and training clergy to meet the needs of both the first generation and the American-born."[363]

3.   Cross-cultural evangelism by diaspora Christians.

As an African pastor living in America who has a passion for cross-cultural evangelism, Abeneazer Gezhegn Urga discusses issues he sees in diaspora Christians being able to engage in cross-cultural evangelism in America.

Urga sees church disunity caused by "personal, ethnic, political, and language divisions," and character issues such as pride, selfish ambition, and competitiveness distracting diaspora Christians from engaging in cross-cultural evangelism.[364] Urga challenges diaspora Christians to learn new languages to reach their neighbors. This involves overcoming the barrier of shyness and being proactive in learning other languages and cultures.[365]

Another major hindrance is fear and/or antagonism towards certain people groups. Urga writes, "Terrorism and other nationalistic

---

[357] Chai, in Warner and Wittner, eds., 300.
[358] Chai, in Warner and Wittner, eds., 319.
[359] Chai, in Warner and Wittner, eds., 306.
[360] Chai, in Warner and Wittner, eds., 306.
[361] George, in Warner and Wittner, eds., 271.
[362] George, in Warner and Wittner, eds., 272.
[363] George, in Warner and Wittner, eds., 290.
[364] Abeneazer Gezahegn Urga, *A Reflection on Diaspora Cross-Cultural Evangelism: An African Perspective,* (Barnes & Noble, 2015), Kindle Locations 227-228.
[365] Urga, Kindle Locations 301-302.

movements against the West, specifically against the United States, have created a climate of fear, hatred, indifference, and Jonah's judgmental mindset among too many American Christians."[366] This can also be applied to other diaspora Christians who have their own prejudices toward certain people groups attributable to past conflicts or wrongs, or due to their own culture's attitudes towards other people groups.

Urga sees pessimism about evangelism efforts, which he calls "Missiopessimism" (the lack of faith and joy in doing evangelism) as a problem in current evangelism ministries.[367] Another issue Urga talks about is the schisms in the diaspora churches.[368] Urga asks whether we are merely doing social work or preaching the gospel in our evangelism?[369] Urga discusses the obstacles he sees for "Diaspora Cross-Cultural Evangelists,"[370] such as the lack of cross-cultural skills, lack of intentionality, loneliness, sexual sin, materialism, and busyness.[371] Urga calls ethnocentrism "the Universal Plague in the Diaspora."[372]

Relational Paradigm

Enoch Wan observes a lack of "relational reality" in Western society today. To support this view, he points to the high mobility in urban cities, high rate of failed marriages and broken/dysfunctional families, virtual relationships through channels like social media instead of personal interaction, the church's focus on programs and ministries to foster numerical growth instead of genuine Christian "body life," and the growing popularity of the "gospel of health and wealth" which he feels lacks relational intensity.[373]

From the lack of genuine relationships in contemporary society and in the church, Wan lists the following reasons for doing diaspora missions through relational paradigm:

First, it is an excellent Christian response to the cry for relationship from people of the twenty-first century. Second, it is a practical way to rediscover "relationship" which is the essence of Christian faith and practice. Third, it has been proven to be effective in ministering to diaspora communities and individuals in need of Christian charity. Fourth, it is a paradigm that enables

---

[366] Urga, Kindle Locations 331-333.
[367] Urga, Kindle Location 364.
[368] Urga, Kindle Locations 454-455.
[369] Urga, Kindle Location 499.
[370] Urga, Kindle Location 593.
[371] Urga, Kindle Locations 593-691.
[372] Urga, Kindle Location 749.
[373] Wan, *Diaspora Missiology: Theory, Methodology, and Practice,* 142.

the synthesizing of diaspora missiology and diaspora missions. Fifth, it is transculturally relevant to societies in the majority world which are highly relational. Sixth, it nurtures a Kingdom orientation and strategically fulfills the Great Commission (a vertical relationship with the Sovereign Lord), and a working relationship with fellow "Kingdom Workers" (horizontally with one another). Seventh, it enables the practice of "strategic stewardship" and "relational accountability." Eighth, in light of the shift of Christendom's center from the West to the majority world, strategic partnership and synergy require the practice of relational paradigm, instead of the traditional paternalist tendency and entrepreneurship of the West.[374]

Here is a summary of Wan's explanation of the theological basis for relational paradigm: man was created in the image of God; man's existence is solely dependent on God at all times; man's ability to know and to undertake in missions is all dependent on God.[375]

Before relational realism was proposed by Wan, Paul G. Hiebert had proposed critical realism to address the problems faced by the Western church due to cultural and religious pluralism.[376] Hiebert warns against complacency in the midst of cultural and religious pluralism and sees that one "of the greatest challenges to Western church is to lay again the theological foundations of the truth of the gospel and to train its members how to proclaim this with humility and love."[377]

Hiebert sees the reason for critical realism is the emerging globalism and explains that critical realist "epistemology strikes a middle ground between positivism, with its emphasis on objective truth, and instrumentalism, with its stress on the subjective nature of human knowledge... It affirms the presence of objective truth but recognizes that this is subjectively apprehended."[378]

Hiebert explains that critical realism is both "realistic" and "critical," because "it assumes a real world that exists independently from human perceptions or opinions" and also "it examines the processes by which humans acquire knowledge and finds that this knowledge does not have a literal one-to-one correspondence to reality."[379]

As opposed to critical realism, which focuses on how uncertain it is for human beings to know reality, relational paradigm sees the reality of the external world is based primarily on the vertical relationship between God and His creation, and secondarily on the horizontal relationship within creation

---

[374] Wan, *Diaspora Missiology: Theory, Methodology, and Practice*, 142.
[375] Wan, *Diaspora Missiology: Theory, Methodology, and Practice*, 143.
[376] Paul G. Hiebert, *Missiological Implications of Epistemological Shifts: Affirming Truth in a Modern/Postmodern World*, (Harrisburg, PA: Trinity Press Int., 1999), 67.
[377] Hiebert, 67.
[378] Hiebert, 69.
[379] Hiebert, 69.

which includes spiritual beings, humans, and nature.[380] Wan sees science can function as a road map and provide human-based paradigm but cannot claim to be the only way to reality and absolute truth.[381]

Wan makes the following points in relational realism: "God is the Truth: His Word (incarnate with personhood, inscripturated and revealed in written form) is truth, His work (creation, redemption, transformation, etc.) is truthful."[382] Relational realism sees truth and reality are "multi-dimensional, multi-level, and multi-contextual" and that all human efforts and disciplines without the vertical relationship with God are "defective ways to approximate truth and reality."[383] In relational realism, truth and reality are best comprehended and experienced in the relational networks of God and the three created orders: 1) angels, 2) humans, and 3) nature.[384]

Wan believes that truth is ultimately seen through the vertical relationship with God because man can be blinded to truth and reality without God and His revelation.[385] Wan writes, "No human judgment is final, nor can it be dogmatic/conclusive; without the vertical relationship to God—the absolute Truth and the most Real."[386]

Wan sees relational paradigm is very relevant cross-culturally and in the majority world "because most societies in the majority world are highly relational in operation, i.e., intricate networks interwoven at multiple levels."[387]

Relational Paradigm in Diaspora Missions

In the article "Missionaries in Our Own Backyard: The Canadian Context," Joel Thiessen sees from his experience the importance of the relationship to God in local mission in Canada. He writes, "First, missionary activity will not occur without church leaders and lay members depending on and being attentive to the Holy Spirit's leading."[388] Thiessen suggests that mission leaders should call believers to slow down their busy lifestyle so they can be more sensitive and connected to God in order to participate in the missionary efforts in Canada.[389]

Relational paradigm has been shown to be successful with immigrant populations. Thiessen observes research studies "continuously reveal successes

---

[380] Wan, *Diaspora Missiology: Theory, Methodology, and Practice*, 144.
[381] Wan, *Diaspora Missiology: Theory, Methodology, and Practice*, 144.
[382] Wan, *Diaspora Missiology: Theory, Methodology, and Practice*, 144.
[383] Wan, *Diaspora Missiology: Theory, Methodology, and Practice*, 144.
[384] Wan, *Diaspora Missiology: Theory, Methodology, and Practice*, 144.
[385] Wan, *Diaspora Missiology: Theory, Methodology, and Practice*, 144.
[386] Wan, *Diaspora Missiology: Theory, Methodology, and Practice*, 144.
[387] Wan, *Diaspora Missiology: Theory, Methodology, and Practice*, 150.
[388] Joel Thiessen, "Missionaries in Our Own Backyard: The Canadian Context," in Craig Ott and J. D. Payne, eds., *Missionary Methods: Research, Reflections, and Realities*, (Pasadena, CA: William Carey Library, 2013),
[389] Thiessen, in Ott and Payne, eds., 136.

around congregations that host ethnic-specific events which enable fellow members of one's ethnic community to share in a common language, food, music, and culture." [390] Furthermore, Thiessen points to many sociological studies where "one of the leading reasons that someone joins a religious group is because they were invited by someone in that group."[391]

Social networking is an application of relational paradigm. In *Scattered Africans Keep Coming*, Edu-Bekoe and Enoch Wan write, "Networking is invaluable in diaspora mission...Various congregations, societies, assemblies of all denominations should 'let the gospel flow in the normal, biblical way in existing social networks' (George Patterson 2010)."[392] The diaspora GPCs (Ghanaian Presbyterian congregations) use networking strictly based on family and friendship.[393]

Relational Missionary Training

Enoch Wan and Mark Hedinger applied "relational paradigm" to missionary training in *Relational Missionary Training: Theology, Theory, and Practice.* They worked on the Trinitarian paradigm in 2006 and Enoch Wan developed "relational paradigm" in several publications since 2006.[394]

Wan and Hedinger cited the five guiding principles for mission training from Wan and Nguyen in "Towards a Theology of Relational Mission Training – An Application of the Relational Paradigm"[395] as follows:

1. Relationship is prominent before, during, and after the training process.
2. The goal of training [is] to build up spiritual Christians who possess and display biblical values.
3. Trainers and trainees create a community of faith in which they fellowship, set examples for one another, and for the world.
4. Spiritual maturity, the outcome of the vertical relationship between God and the trainer and trainees, is the primary objective of mission training. Holiness is the most important qualification of God's servants.
5. Only spiritual trainers can produce spiritual trainees.

---

[390] Thiessen, in Ott and Payne, eds., 138.

[391] Thiessen, in Ott and Payne, eds., 138.

[392] Yaw Attah Edu-Bekoe and Enoch Wan, *Scattered Africans Keep Coming: A Case Study of Diaspora Missiology on Ghanaian Diaspora and Congregations in the USA,* (Portland, OR: Institute of Diaspora studies-USA, 2013), 176.

[393] Edu-Bekoe and Wan, 176.

[394] Enoch Wan and Mark Hedinger, *Relational Missionary Training: Theology, Theory, and Practice,* (Skyforest, CA: Urban Loft Publishers, 2017), 12.

[395] Wan and Hedinger, 92, citing Enoch Wan and Tin V. Nguyen. "Towards a Theology of Relational Mission Training – An Application of the Relational Paradigm Enoch Wan and Tin V. Nguyen" *Global Missiology* English 2:11 (11-12, 2013).

Wan and Hedinger list seven key missionary relationships: 1) Relationships within the Trinity, 2) Relationships between the Trinity and the missionary that he sends to the nations, 3) Relationships between the Trinity and the audience, 4) Relationships between the missionary and the audience, 5) Relationships between the missionary and his/her home culture, 6) Relationships between the audience and his/her culture, and 7) An appropriate relationship with evil spirits.[396]

Wan and Hedinger explain for #7 that "the only appropriate relationship for a believer of any culture with those evil beings is to recognize their wiles, actively choose God and His ways, and flee from the evil one."[397]

Based on the relational paradigm, "mission skills, attitudes, knowledge are designed for and evaluated on the basis of relational outcomes."[398] The following are all relational in relational missionary training: content of teaching/learning, context of teaching/learning, methods of teaching/learning, the task of mission, and the desired training outcomes.[399]

The goal of relational paradigm is to have healthy and appropriate relationships with each other and with the Triune God.[400] Relational missionary training measures the outcome by the relationships between the various parties involved, which means that "one person can do all that is 'right' and still not see the goals accomplished."[401]

Most importantly, Wan and Hedinger see that the goal of mission training is the transformation of everyone involved. They write that "the training of missionaries seeks transformation, and that sort of desired outcome is far from mechanical or technical."[402] Transformation occurs through the interaction of vertical relationships and horizontal relationships.[403]

Chinese Culture and Relational Paradigm

The relational paradigm is very relevant to Chinese culture, which is seen basically as concrete relational.[404] This is referring to their way of thinking through concrete experiences. Hesselgrave observes, "Confucius' emphasis on tradition, ritual, and social relationships was certainly in accord with concrete relational thinking from the first."[405]

---

[396] Wan and Hedinger, 284-285.
[397] Wan and Hedinger, 285.
[398] Wan and Hedinger, 290.
[399] Wan and Hedinger, 290.
[400] Wan and Hedinger, 291.
[401] Wan and Hedinger, 291.
[402] Wan and Hedinger, 293.
[403] Wan and Hedinger, 293.
[404] David J. Hesselgrave, *Communicating Christ Cross-Culturally: An Introduction to Missionary Communication*, 2nd ed. (Grand Rapids, MI: Zondervan, 1991), 328.
[405] Hesselgrave, 328.

Hesselgrave defines concrete relational thinking as "people who attempt to discover truth in such a way that life and reality are seen pictorially in terms of active emotional relationships present in a concrete situation."[406] Concrete relational thinkers use symbols, stories, events, and objects instead of general propositions and principles in verbal communication.[407] Hesselgrave sees the Chinese are "especially prone to rely on nonverbal communication of all types – gesture and sign language, music and the plastic arts, ritual and drama, and image projection."[408]

In relating to the Chinese, one needs to be aware of how they approach decision making. Hesselgrave notes, "Some cultures place a great value on decisiveness and 'making up one's mind' as soon as possible. *Any* decision is deemed to be better than *no* decision."[409] Other cultures do not see making a decision is always necessary and can live "with a degree of indecisiveness."[410] Hesslegrave writes:

> The Chinese are encouraged to postpone as long as possible any decision regarding the future course of action. When they do make such a decision, it will usually be with a high degree of tentativeness. To the Chinese it is wise to keep one's options open in case the situation changes. It is *virtuous* to change one's mind if the situation does change![411]

Enoch Wan sees that Chinese culture tries hard to avoid confrontation at all times and at all cost. People try to protect each other from losing face or losing the relationship.[412] From these common traits, we see that the value of relationships for Chinese people is woven into the culture. Thus, the relational paradigm is very applicable to the Chinese context.

We can see the relational paradigm being practiced in the successful outreaches in China. In the article "Christian Witness to the Chinese People," Thomas Wang and Sharon Chan write, "Invasion from the West in past centuries has left Chinese people with deep suspicions about Christianity."[413] However they see "incarnational servanthood" as an effective approach through placing mature Christian professionals and business people in China. They write, "There these people make significant professional and economical contributions to the

---

[406] Hesselgrave, 325.
[407] Hesselgrave, 325.
[408] Hesselgrave, 325.
[409] Hesselgrave, 613.
[410] Hesselgrave, 614.
[411] Hesselgrave, 614.
[412] Wan, "Mission among the Chinese Diaspora - A case study of migration & mission," <http://www.enochwan.com/english/articles/pdf/Mission%20among%20the%20Chinese%20Dia spora.pdf≥ (February 17, 2013).
[413] Thomas Wang and Sharon Chan, "Christian Witness to the Chinese People," in *Perspectives on the World Christian Movement: A Reader*, 3rd ed. (Pasadena, CA: William Carey Library, 1999), 643.

country while at the same time rubbing shoulders on a regular basis with their Chinese counterparts, many of whom are government officials."[414]

Summary

This section discussed the historical development, historical perspective, theological background, and current issues in diaspora missiology. Diaspora missiology can be traced back to the 1970s in the Lausanne Conference and has been gaining more attention in missionary conferences. The Bible is also filled with the theme of migration. Christianity has been spreading through migration throughout its history. The brief history of different diasporas shows us the work of God in bringing the gospel to and through diaspora. The relational paradigm and application to diaspora missions were discussed. The relational paradigm offers an effective missionary strategy in ministering to diaspora. Diaspora missions and relational paradigm are both ways to engage in missions to, by, and with diaspora people. We see that the value of relationships for Chinese people is woven into the culture. Thus, the relational paradigm is very applicable for Chinese Christian diaspora to engage in diaspora cross-cultural missions.

---

[414] Wang and Chan, 643.

CHAPTER 4
LOCAL CROSSCULTURAL MINISTRY OF CHINESE CONGREGATIONS IN THE SAN FRANCISCO BAY AREA

Introduction

This study looked at Chinese churches in the SFBA founded from 1853 to 2006 based on the churches listed in *The Bay Area Chinese Churches Research Project Phase II*. Co-author Lei found a total of one hundred ninety-five churches listed in the report (the report itself states there are one hundred ninety-four churches in 2008).[415] Lei found one hundred forty-two accessible church websites (73% of the total churches). Please see Figure 3. Twenty-nine churches had no website. Nineteen website addresses were not valid or not accessible. Five churches used their denomination website and did not have their own website page. Lei found three churches which were inactive or dissolved or merged. These websites were accessed from 5/10/2016 to 1/12/2017.

Accessible church websites	142
No websites	29
Invalid address/not able to access	19
Denomination websites	5
Total churches studied	195

Figure 1 Church website summary

---

[415] Chuck and Tseng, eds., 10.

Church is inactive/dissolved/merged	3

Figure 2 Church that is inactive/dissolved/merged

Archival Research

Louise Corti's SAGE encyclopedia defines archival research as "the locating, evaluating, and systematic interpretation and analysis of sources found in archives." [416] SAGE dictionary defines archival research as "research that involves review of records or documents in archives."[417] Enoch Wan, in his handout on archival research, defines archival research as a type of primary research.[418]

Internet Research

Internet research is a recent research phenomenon and is developing rapidly.[419] One of the biggest challenges of online research is the ethical and legal complexity of the internet.[420] Books that introduce internet research methods include: *The Internet Handbook* (O'Dochartaigh 2001), *Internet Research Methods* (Hewson, Yule, Laurent, and Vogel 2002), and *Online Research Essentials* (Russell and Purcell 2009).[421]

Case Study

Case Studies Background

Case study research is "a qualitative approach in which the investigator explores a real-life, contemporary bounded system (a *case*) or multiple bounded systems (cases) over time, through detailed, in-depth data collection involving *multiple sources of information* (e.g., observations, interviews, audiovisual material, and documents and reports), and reports a *case description* and *case themes.*"[422]

---

[416] Louise Corti, "Archival Research," <http://srmo.sagepub.com/view/the-sage-encyclopedia-of-social-science-research-methods/n20.xml≥ (4/18/2016).
[417] SAGE Knowledge. Dictionary entry for "Archival Research," Class handout from Western Seminary DIS725, Spring 2015.
[418] Enoch Wan, "(10) ARCHIVAL RESEARACH," Class handout from Western Seminary DIS725, Spring 2015.
[419] Tristram Hooley, John Marriott, and Jane Wellens, *What is Online Research? Using the Internet for Social Science Research,* (New York, NY: Bloomsbury Academic, 2012), 7.
[420] Hooley, Marriott, and Wellens, 3.
[421] Hooley, Marriott, and Wellens, 5.
[422] Hooley, Marriott, and Wellens, 97.

Robert K. Yin views a case study as an empirical inquiry that "investigates a contemporary phenomenon within its real-life context."[423] Robert E. Stake assesses that case study can be both qualitative and quantitative. He uses an example of a physician studying a child who is ill. In this example, the physician's record will be more quantitative than qualitative.[424] Stake writes, "In many professional and practical fields, cases are studied and recorded. As a form of research, case study is defined by interest in individual cases, not by the methods of inquiry used."[425]

In an intrinsic case study, it is undertaken to better understand a particular case. In an instrumental case study, it is commenced for providing insight into an issue or to refine a theory.[426] A collective case study is when the researcher studies a number of cases jointly to study a phenomenon, population, or generation condition.[427] The Ark Baptist Church and Forerunner Christian Church case studies were instrumental case studies to provide insight into the cross-cultural ministries of Chinese churches in the SFBA.

Yin perceives a case study will rely on multiple sources of evidence and the data need to converge in a triangulating fashion.[428] According to Yin, "the case study as a research strategy comprises an all-encompassing method—with the logic of design incorporating specific approaches to data collection and to data analysis."[429] Therefore, to Yin "the case study is not either a data collection tactic or merely a design feature alone (Stoecker, 1991) but a comprehensive research strategy."[430]

There are four types of triangulation in doing evaluations: 1) data sources (data triangulation), 2) among different evaluators (investigator triangulation), 3) perspectives on the same data set (theory triangulation), and 4) methods (methodological triangulation).[431]

In the multiple sources of evidence of a case study, there are 1) Archival records, 2) Documents, 3) Observations (direct and participant), 4) Structured interviews and surveys, 5) Focused interviews, and 6) Open-ended interviews.[432]

---

[423] Robert K. Yin, *Case Study Research: Design and Methods*, 2nd ed. (Thousand Oaks, CA: Sage Publications, 1994), 13.
[424] Robert E. Stake, "Case Studies," in Norman K. Denzin and Yvonna S. Lincoln, eds., *Handbook of Qualitative Research*, (Thousand Oaks, CA: Sage Publications, 1995), 236.
[425] Stake, in Denzin and Lincoln, eds., 236.
[426] Stake, in Denzin and Lincoln, eds., 237.
[427] Stake, in Denzin and Lincoln, eds., 237.
[428] Yin, 13.
[429] Yin, 13.
[430] Yin, 13.
[431] Yin, 92.
[432] Yin, 93.

Case Study Field Research

Case study field research was conducted on two Chinese churches in SFBA. The first was a medium size church and the second a large size church. The case study research on the first church was conducted through emails to acquire information as well as face to face conversations. The case study research on the second church was undertaken through phone interviews and emails to obtain information.

Internet Field Research

This study includes internet research, which is a recent research phenomenon and is developing rapidly.[1] However, one of the biggest challenges which online researchers face is the ethical and legal complexity of the internet.[2] There are introductions to the area of online research methods: *The Internet Handbook,*[433] *Internet Research Methods,*[434] and *Online Research Essential.*[435] In the *SAGE Handbook of Online Research Methods,*[436] there is a section on "The internet as an archival resource," with chapters on "The Provision of Access to Quantitative Data for Secondary Analysis" and "Secondary Qualitative Analysis Using Internet Resources." This study used internet research as a primary research by analyzing the data collected from the church websites. Internet research was also used in the Ark Baptist Church case study for the church history and vision.

How the Churches are Started

Figure 5 shows how the churches were started. The information was acquired from the church website or from *The Bay Area Chinese Churches Research Project Phase II* if the church website did not have the information. One church was started by an American person. One by Chinese American families with support from an American church. One by members from an American church. Two churches were started by a Chinese Mission organization. Three by American church missionaries. Four churches were started as American

---

[1] Tristram Hooley, John Marriott, Jane Wellens. *What is online research?,* 7.

[2] Hooley, Marriott, Wellens, *What is online research?,* 3.

[433] Niall O. O'Dochartaigh, *The Internet Research Handbook: A Practical Guide for Students and Researchers in the Social Sciences*, First edition. (London   ; Thousand Oaks, Calif: SAGE Publications Ltd, 2001).

[434] Claire Hewson et al., *Internet Research Methods: A Practical Guide for the Social and Behavioural Sciences* (Sage Publications Ltd, 2003).

[435] Brenda Russell and John Purcell, *Online Research Essentials: Designing and Implementing Research Studies*, 1 edition. (San Francisco: Jossey-Bass, 2009).

[436] Nigel G. Fielding, Raymond M. Lee, and Grant Blank, eds., *The SAGE Handbook of Online Research Methods*, 1 edition. (Los Angeles: SAGE Publications Ltd, 2008).

churches. Five by members from a Chinese church. Co-author Lei was unable to determine how twelve of the churches were started. Twenty-two were Chinese/Taiwanese church plants. Twenty-two churches were started by immigrants or students' families. Twenty-eight were started by an American church or denomination. Thirty-nine churches were started by a Chinese pastor or elder. The highest cases (27%) were started by a Chinese pastor or elder. The second highest cases (19%) were started by an American church or denomination.

Started by Chinese pastor/elder	39
American church/denomination plant	28
Chinese/Taiwanese church plant	22
Started by immigrants/students (families)	22
Started by members from a Chinese church	5
Started as American church	4
Started by American church missionary	3
Started by Chinese Mission organization	2
Started by overseas church	2
Started by an American person	1
Started by Chinese American families	1
Started by members from American church	1
Unable to determine	12

Figure 3 How churches are started

English Worship

There is potential for cross-cultural ministry when the Chinese church has English worship. Co-author Lei found one hundred fourteen churches with English worship, seven churches with no English worship, and twenty-one churches with bilingual Chinese/English worship.

English Worship	114
No English Worship	7
Bilingual English worship	21

Figure 4 English worship

English Website

For non-Chinese readers, an English website would be necessary for them to access church information. An English website may include websites with bilingual Chinese and English language. When a website is totally Chinese and the navigation bars are all in Chinese, then it was listed as "No English website." One hundred thirty-one churches had English website (92%). Eleven churches had no English website (8%). Many of the churches had a separate English website.

English website	131
No English website	11

Figure 5 English website

Local Cross–Cultural Ministries

Co-author Lei looked through the church websites for mention of potential cross-cultural ministries. While many of the ministries in the Chinese church serve Chinese speakers, they also have ministries that may be cross-cultural, especially ministries by the English congregation.

Church Internal Ministries

Co-author Lei found seven churches that mentioned Awana. Thirty-one mentioned VBS. VBS included kids cooking summer camp and VBS in San Diego. Sixteen churches mentioned sports ministry. The sports mentioned were: Tai Chi, ping pong, basketball camp, open gym (basketball, badminton, and volleyball), ping-pong tournament, children's soccer, table tennis, volleyball tournament, and picnic.

Awana	7
VBS	31
Sports ministry	16

Figure 6 Church internal ministries

Food Bank and Homeless Ministry

Co-author Lei found eighteen churches which mentioned participating in local Food Bank ministry. The Food bank mentioned was "Second Harvest." Thirteen churches mentioned participating in homeless ministry.

Food Bank	18

Homeless ministry	13

Figure 7 Food Bank and Homeless ministry

Refugee Ministry

Co-author Lei found three churches which mentioned refugee ministry on their website. Laotian and Nepalese refugee ministries were mentioned.

Refugee ministry	3

Figure 8 Refugee ministry

Senior Ministry

Co-author Lei found fourteen churches which mentioned senior ministry. These ministries include senior's home, senior activity center, senior academy, and senior lunch. This also included caroling at senior homes.

Senior ministry	14

Figure 9 Senior ministry

Financial Support for Local Ministries

Co-author Lei found seven churches which mentioned financial support for local ministries – such as mission organization (YWAM, BJM), seminary, church, and evangelism ministries. Six churches mentioned financial support of college campus ministry.

Financial support local ministry (i.e. mission, seminary, church, evangelism)	7
Financial support college campus ministry	6

Figure 10 Financial support of local ministry

Different Language Ministry

Co-author Lei found one church had a Hispanic ministry, one had an Indonesian service, and one helped to birth several different language ministries.

Hispanic ministry	1
Indonesian service	1
Helping birth several different language ministries	1

Figure 11 Different language ministry

Church Outreach

Co-author Lei found different church outreach programs and ministries. Five churches mentioned community cooking classes. One mentioned a community children's choir. Twenty-four churches mentioned various community outreach activities at the church. Church community outreaches mentioned: caroling, carpenter fun shop, Christmas outreach, summer BBQ, community center, special events for the church and community during special holidays, Easter egg hunt, evangelistic conference, free laptops, tax preparation, seminars, Hallelujah party, Goodwill truck, Harvest festival, relationship seminar, women's tea, health and parenting seminars, restaurant fellowship, community center, karaoke, Saturday Coffee Corner, hiking, serve meals, Thanksgiving dinner, Christmas service, Toastmasters, and Warriors Fellowship night. One church mentioned high school dance competition. One mentioned counseling center. One mentioned social connecting. One mentioned knitting. One mentioned alpha course. One mentioned piano and knitting classes. One mentioned book sale/holiday bazaar/concerts. Two churches mentioned line dancing. Six mentioned music/art classes. Seven mentioned Chinese school. While many of these church outreach programs may target Chinese peoples, these have the potential to reach and serve non-Chinese as well.

Church community outreach	24
Chinese school (may include non-Chinese attendee)	7
Music/Art class	6
Community cooking class	5
Line dancing	2
Community children's choir	1
High school Dance Competition	1
Counseling center	1
Social connecting	1
Knitting	1
Alpha course	1
Piano, knitting class	1
Book Sale/Holiday Bazaar/concerts	1

Figure 12 Church outreach

Local Mission and Evangelism

The churches had local missions and evangelism training. Seven churches mentioned local evangelism training. This training included: City Impact conference and Evangelism Explosion. Two churches mentioned Native American ministry. One mentioned Jesus Loves Chinatown local short-term mission and street evangelism. Four churches mentioned local mission trips. Local mission trips mentioned were to Las Vegas, San Diego, San Francisco, Oakland, and Sacramento. Eight churches mentioned local missions. Local missions mentioned included Atwater, San Francisco Bay Area, Baja California, Miami, Fresno California, inner city mission, disaster response, Memphis Tennessee, and New Orleans. Two churches mentioned campus evangelism. Campus evangelism included San Jose State outreach. Some of these ministries may only serve or impact Chinese people; they may also serve or impact non-Chinese.

Local mission	8
Local Evangelism training	7
Local mission trip	4
Native American ministry (Duckwater)	2
Campus evangelism	2
Jesus Loves Chinatown local short-term mission/Street Evangelism	1

Figure 13 Local mission and evangelism

City Ministry

Co-author Lei found churches that mentioned participation in city ministry. These ministries would most likely be cross-cultural in nature. Twelve churches mentioned participating in City Team ministry. City Team included canned food drives and homeless ministry. Four churches mentioned participating in City Impact ministry. Two mentioned social justice ministry. The social justice ministry mentioned is a program for overcoming poverty. Two churches mentioned CityServe/compassion network. One mentioned inner-city ministry. One mentioned social justice activism.

City Team	12
City Impact	4
Social justice ministry	2
CityServe/compassion network	2
Inner city ministry	1

Social justice activism	1

Figure 14 City ministry

Joint Outreach with Other Churches

Joint outreach with other churches may be a cross-cultural experience. Eight churches mentioned joint outreach with other churches. Joint outreach with other churches included Building Bridges community service and mission, church planting, Vietnamese, Spanish, and Cambodian churches met in the building, and outreach with YWAM.

Joint outreach with other churches	8

Figure 15 Joint outreach with other churches

Community Service

Many churches mentioned community service. Two churches mentioned Habitat for Humanity. Twelve mentioned children/youth community services. Children/youth community services include: Boy scout/girl scout, camp, pre-school, Kid's club, Summer Youth Choir camp, tutoring/mentor service, Youth Volunteer corps, and volunteer in elementary school. One church mentioned sweeping city streets. Eleven mentioned community education service. Community education service included: disadvantaged behavioral kids, after school program, after-school English/Chinese program, developmentally disabled program, Chinese class, and tutoring in math and English. Fifteen churches mentioned different kinds of community service. These community services included: Salvation Army toy drive, donate school supplies, toys, health care for people in need, Angel Tree, Mothers of preschoolers, health screening and education, donate pillows for cancer patients, dental seminar, eye care for kids, food for others mobile packing, teach board games to 3rd-6th graders in elementary school, free tax prep, help elderly, disabled, single parent, deployed military and veteran, or otherwise overwhelmed households with minor maintenance, repair, or visitation projects, immigration advocates, legal service, pack food, special needs children support, and ministry meeting the needs of poor and hungry in the North Oakland area. One church mentioned hospital work. One mentioned shoe pantry. Two churches mentioned special needs children. Two churches mentioned Sacred Heart and Family Giving Tree.

Community service (others)	15
Children/Youth Community services	12
Community Education service	11
Habitat for Humanity	2
Special needs children	2
Sacred Heart, Family Giving Tree	2
Sweep city streets	1
Hospital work	1
Shoe pantry	1

Figure 16 Community service

New Immigrant/ESL

Co-author Lei found six churches which mentioned new immigrant ministry and eight churches which mentioned ESL ministry. These ministries included: translation service, citizenship class, parenting class, American customs and etiquette class, and English conversation outreach.

New immigrant ministry	6
ESL	8

Figure 17 New immigrant/ESL

Neighborhood Outreach

Co-author Lei found eleven churches which mentioned neighborhood outreach. Neighborhood outreach included: Local outreach Sunday, handing out Father's love letters and popcorn, ministering, and invitation to the movie night, volunteer in booth at a Chinese festival, lawn Christmas outreach, Project Love in SF, and food box delivery. Ten churches mentioned neighborhood activities. Neighborhood activities included: AIDS ride, Alpha pregnancy center, Freedom House, Angle Tree, Bay Area Chinese Emergency Relief, caroling, community car show, host Christmas dinner at the community center, Neighbor fund small business development, New year gift baskets, and See you at the poles. One church mentioned prayer walk. One mentioned visiting the fire-station.

Neighborhood outreach	11
Neighborhood activities	10
Prayer walk	1

| Visit fire-station | 1 |

Figure 18 Neighborhood outreach

Women's Ministries

Co-author Lei found two churches that mentioned women's recovery ministry. Women's recovery ministry included help for women leaving prostitution. One church mentioned sexual abuse recovery ministry. One mentioned female minister association. The female minister association does community service, evangelism, and Bible study. One church mentioned unplanned pregnancy ministry. One mentioned human trafficking ministry.

Women's recovery	2
Sexual abuse recovery	1
Female minister association	1
Unplanned pregnancy	1
Human trafficking	1

Figure 19 Women's ministries

Facebook

Many of the churches had a link to their Facebook page on their website. The Facebook page may mention the church's community activities. However, no data from churches' Facebook pages were included in this study.

Other Ministries

Co-author Lei found other ministries mentioned such as Medical/health ministry (five churches). Medical/health ministry included combating addictions. There were also mentioned ministries for American troops (one church), Native Americans (one church), and foster home (one church).

Medical/Health ministry	5
American Troops	1
Native Americans	1
Foster home	1

Figure 20 Other ministries

Top Ministries

These were the top ten ministries mentioned by the church websites: 1) VBS, 2) Church community outreach, 3) Food Bank, 4) Sports ministry, 5) Community service (others), 6) Seniors ministry, 7) Homeless ministry, 8) City Team, 9) Children/Youth Community services, 10) Community Education service.

1	VBS	31
2	Church community outreach	24
3	Food Bank	18
4	Sports ministry	16
5	Community service (others)	15
6	Senior ministry	14
7	Homeless ministry	13
8	City Team	12
9	Children/Youth Community services	12
10	Community Education service	11

Figure 21 Top 10 ministries

Summary

The website research yielded valuable information about the ministries conducted by Chinese churches in outreach and community service. While many of the ministries targeted Chinese people, there were many ministries that were cross-cultural or have the potential to be cross-cultural. The majority of the churches had English or bilingual worship services and websites. This is a good starting point to engage in cross-cultural ministry. The research shows that the Chinese churches in the SFBA were well-positioned for cross-cultural ministry and were already engaging in local cross-cultural ministry. Many Chinese churches were actively involved in community service. They had found many ways to use the church building in outreach to the community. Since churches typically don't post every activity or ministry on their website, what the website research shows is likely only a partial list of the local ministries by Chinese churches in SFBA. However, the potential of turning Chinese outreach ministries into cross-cultural outreach ministries is great, such as sports, art, music, and educational ministries.

Co-author Lei found most of the cross-cultural ministry activities from the English ministry websites of the Chinese churches. This shows that most of the cross-cultural community service activities were done by the English-speaking congregation members of the Chinese churches. American-born or American-raised Chinese may feel more comfortable and interested in the community service activities than their Chinese parents because of their fluency in English and growing up in a multi-cultural environment. Chinese churches can recognize this and encourage their English congregation members in community involvement. The purpose of this study was to encourage the Chinese diaspora Christians to be more engaged in cross-cultural ministries, not merely for the second generation American-born or American-raised Chinese to be engaged in serving the community. Local cross-cultural ministries should be a part of the ministry of both the Chinese and English congregations in Chinese churches in the SFBA.

CHAPTER 5
CONEXTUALIZATION OF DIASPORA MISSION AND CROSS-CULTURAL TRAINING FOR CHINESE DIASPORA IN THE SAN FRANCISCO BAY AREA

Introduction

For Chinese Christian diaspora to engage in cross-cultural ministries, the authors perceive that cross-cultural training is needed. The authors also observe that contextualization of cross-cultural ministries for Chinese diaspora would be helpful. Winter notes that "*most non-Christians in the world today are not culturally near neighbors of any Christians and that it will take a special kind of 'cross-cultural' evangelism to reach them.*"[437]

Winter gives the example of the Christian church in Pakistan to illustrate this problem. Even though there are hundreds of thousands of Christians in Pakistan, the country is still 97 percent Muslim. Christians are not "culturally near" enough to the Muslims for Christians to witness to them in the same way as someone from their own culture.[438] Another example is the Church of South India, where "95 per cent of its members come from only five out of the more than 100 social classes (castes) in South India."[439] This means that the Christian church in South India has not reached most of the social classes or cultural groups in their area.

---

[437] Ralph D. Winter, "The New Macedonia: A Revolutionary New Era in Mission Begins," in Ralph D. Winter and Steven C. Hawthorne, eds., *Perspectives on the World Christian Movement: A Reader*, 3rd ed (Pasadena, CA: William Carey Library, 1999), 340.
[438] Winter, in Winter and Hawthorne, eds., 340.
[439] Winter, in Winter and Hawthorne, eds., 340.

Winter uses Taiwan as an example to show what E-1, E-2, E-3 evangelism means. There are four major groups of people in Taiwan: 1) the Minnans who came from mainland China before the Mandarin-speaking people, 2) the Hakka-speaking people who came earlier from mainland China than the Minnans, 3) the Mandarin speaking people who came from mainland China, 4) the few hundred thousand aboriginal peoples who speak Malayo-Polynesian dialects that are entirely different from Chinese. E-1 evangelism occurs when a Mainlander Chinese Christian evangelizes someone from the mainland. E-2 evangelism occurs if a Mainlander Chinese Christian evangelizes a Minnan Taiwanese or a Hakka. E-3 evangelism occurs if the Mainlander Chinese Christian evangelizes someone from the aboriginal people. E-3 is more complex because it involves a greater cultural distance.[440] As a side note, many of the aboriginal people in Taiwan are now Christians. The Operation Mobilization (OM) website reports over 64% Taiwan Aborigines identity themselves as Christian.[441]

Winter observes that the "Samaria" in Acts 1:8 is not referring to geographical distance, rather cultural distance, because Samaria is not that far away geographically. Winter points to Jesus passing through Samaria when He travels from Galilee to Jerusalem. Even though Jesus can communicate with the Samaritan woman in the same language, there are significant cultural differences between the Jews and Samaritans, such as the way they worship God.[442] Winter also sees that the various nations listed on the day of Pentecost "were for the most part not *countries* but *peoples*."[443] He sees in the Great Commission the phrase "make disciples of all *ethne* (peoples)" means that God wants not simply all countries but all peoples to be disciples.[444]

E-2 evangelism is a good starting point for Christians to get involved in cross-cultural ministry. In E-2 evangelism we don't need to learn another language. We need to be willing to reach someone who is not the same culturally or ethnically from us. E-2 can also be called "local" cross-cultural ministry. E-3 evangelism is the next step in cross-cultural ministry. Winter sees E-3 as being part of the "uttermost part of the earth" in Acts 1:8. The people in E-3 evangelism would be very different from us in their culture and language.[445] E-3 would involve going overseas or to more distant places such being a cross-cultural missionary.

---

[440] Winter, in Winter and Hawthorne, eds., 341.
[441] OM, "Religion," <https://www.omusa.org/areas/country/taiwan> (3/31/2017)
[442] Winter, in Winter and Hawthorne, eds., 343.
[443] Winter, in Winter and Hawthorne, eds., 346.
[444] Winter, in Winter and Hawthorne, eds., 346.
[445] Winter, in Winter and Hawthorne, eds., 344.

Cultural Differences

The first place to start in cross-cultural ministry training is to understand the cultural differences among people in the world. First of all, what is culture? Grunlan and Mayers give the definition of culture as "learned and shared attitudes, values, and ways of behaving" and "includes the material artifacts created by the members of a cultural group."[446] Another definition of culture is "a system of meanings and values that shape one's behavior."[447] Charles H. Kraft views culture as "the nonbiological, nonenvironmental reality in which humans live."[448] Geert H. Hofstede views culture as *the collective programming of the mind that distinguishes the members of one group or category of people from another.*"[449]

Hofstede sees there are three levels of human mental programming: individual, collective, and universal.[450] He observes that each person's "mental programming is partly unique, partly shared with others."[451] The universal level is shared by all or almost all humans. The collective level is shared with people belonging to a certain group or category. The individual level of human programming is unique for each person.[452] Culture refers to the collective level of human mental programming, which is learned and shared with people who have gone through the same learning processes.[453]

Each culture has its own ideal behaviors, accepted behaviors, and unacceptable behaviors. When the accepted behavior is close to the ideals of the culture, the culture is seen as static, whereas if the accepted behavior is further from the ideals of the culture, the culture is seen as dynamic.[454] In order to understand ourselves and others, "we must understand the influence of our culture on every aspect of who we are, how we think, how we interpret our experiences and what we value."[455]

---

[446] Stephen A. Grunlan and Marvin K. Mayers, *Cultural Anthropology: A Christian Perspective,* 2nd ed. (Grand Rapids, MI: Zondervan Publishing House, 1988), 39.

[447] Lane, 16. This is taken from Larke Nahme Huang and Sara Nieves-Grafals, "Cross-Cultural Counseling" (lecture given at the National Multicultural Institute, Washington, D.C., November 3-4, 1994).

[448] Charles H. Kraft, *Christianity in Culture: A Study in Biblical Theologizing in Cross-Cultural Perspective,* (Maryknoll, NY: Orbis, 2005), 37.

[449] Geert H. Hofstede, *Culture's Consequences: Comparing Values, Behaviors, Institutions, and Organizations Across Nations,* 2nd ed. (Thousand Oaks, CA: Sage Publications, Inc., 2001), 9.

[450] Hofstede, 3.

[451] Hofstede, 2.

[452] Hofstede, 2.

[453] Hofstede, 3.

[454] Lane, 32-33.

[455] Lane, 34.

The Dimensions of Culture

Social scientists have identified different dimensions of cultures that can be useful to understand the differences between the cultures. Patty Lane, in *A Beginner's Guide to Crossing Cultures,* describes the cultural dimensions of context, activity, authority, relationship, and time. We also look at the worldviews and cultural values of different cultures.[456]

Context

Cultures can be divided into high and low context.[457] Low context cultures do not place as high of an importance on the context compared to high context cultures.[458] Context can include the physical environment, the way the person expresses themselves through body language, facial expression, and tone of voice, and the way people appear, such as their clothes and jewelry. It can also include the way things are done or the process of how things are done.[459]

The characteristics of a high context culture are: the context of an event is as important as the event itself, the listener is responsible for understanding what the speaker intends to communicate, the person and idea that is communicated is not separated, experience is as valuable as the fact, and life is viewed as a whole.[460]

The characteristics of a low context culture are: the content is more important than the context, the speaker is responsible to make the communication understood by the listener, people are defined by their recent achievements, and analytical thinking is preferred.[461]

Many Asian countries, such as Japan and Korea, are high context cultures.[462] The dominant U.S. culture is low context. In the U.S., important agreements can be made regardless of the settings, even on golf courses, in saunas, or over lunch. This would not be appropriate in high context cultures. In high context cultures, there is a setting for people to develop relationship, such as over a meal or drink. However, it is not the place to make the actual formal agreements.[463] In low context cultures, communication mainly involves the content. However, in high context cultures, it is not only the content but also other things that are involved in the way things are communicated. Usually we don't need to "read between the lines" in low context cultures and the

---

[456] Lane, 47.
[457] Lane, 48.
[458] Lane, 48.
[459] Lane, 48-49.
[460] Lane, 49. Lane referenced Jaime S. Wurzel and Nancy K. Fischman, *A Different Place: The Intercultural Classroom* (Newtonville, MA.: Intercultural Resource Corporation, 1994), 38-43.
[461] Lane, 56. Lane referenced Wurzel and Fischman, 38-43.
[462] Lane, 51.
[463] Lane, 57.

communication can be more direct. However, we need to be sensitive in high context cultures to the way people communicate and we need to be aware of what is being communicated in addition to the pure content.

Activity

Another dimension of culture is how a culture sees its activity. In "Doing" cultures, the people value results and materialism. In "Being" cultures, the people value relationships and quality of life.[464]

Based on research, countries with "Doing" cultures are: China,** Japan, Venezuela,* Italy, Ireland, Great Britain, Philippines, United States,* New Zealand, Greece, Argentina, Canada, Belgium, India, Hong Kong, Australia,* South Africa, Colombia, Germany,* Mexico, Switzerland, Austria, and Russia.**[465]

Countries listed as "Being" cultures include: Pakistan, Brazil, Israel, Taiwan, France, Peru, Portugal, Finland, Denmark, Norway, Sweden, Netherlands, Yugoslavia, Chile,* Thailand, Spain, Iran, Turkey, and Singapore.[466]

By knowing the "Doing" and "Being" cultures, it helps us better understand how people value their activities. For the "Doing" cultures, we see they value activities that produce results. For the "Being" cultures, we see they value activities that improve and build up relationships.[467] We can focus on result-oriented activities with the "Doing" cultures and focus on relationship building activities with "Being" cultures.

Lane notes that the U.S. culture's friendliness is "a shallow friendliness that can be very dependent on circumstances."[468] Those in "Being" cultures would treat friendship as a lifelong commitment to be there for each other, not merely to share a common activity.[469] We don't need to judge whether the "Doing" culture or the "Being" culture is good for developing friendships. However, we should respect the way the people of different cultures value their activities and understand the way people make friends is different.

---

[464] Lane, 61.
[465] Lane, 71. Lane referenced research from Hofstede, 315. *These country categories changed during further research conducted by Denise Rotondo Fernandez, Dawn S. Carlson, Lee P. Stepina, and Joel D. Nicholson in "Hofstede's Country Classification 25 Years Later," *Journal of Social Psychology* 137:1 (1997), 43. **These countries were added in more recent research.
[466] Lane, 71. Lane referenced research from Hofstede, 315. *These country categories changed during further research conducted by Fernandez, Carlson, Stepina, and Nicholson in "Hofstede's Country Classification 25 Years Later," *Journal of Social Psychology* 137:1 (1997), 43. **These countries were added in more recent research.
[467] Lane, 63-64.
[468] Lane, 66.
[469] Lane, 66.

Authority

In the authority dimension of cultures, there are two kinds: 1) egalitarian/informal and 2) hierarchical/formal.[470] In egalitarian cultures, all persons have equal value and equal rights. However, a culture may be egalitarian in its values yet not treat each person equally. For example, the United States is an egalitarian culture; nevertheless, there are many in the United States who have experienced discrimination or unequal treatment.[471] In hierarchical cultures, people are expected to be treated differently. It is perceived as appropriate to treat people differently based on factors such as age, gender, race, or caste.[472]

One aspect of the authority dimension is "uncertainty avoidance."[473] Hofstede sees this as "related to the level of stress in a society in the face of an unknown future."[474] Hofstede writes, "Different societies have adapted to uncertainty in different ways. These ways differ not only between traditional and modern societies; but also among modern societies."[475] In cultures with high uncertainty avoidance, the people are not comfortable with ambiguous situations. These cultures are also more hierarchical and formal.[476] On the other hand, the cultures with low uncertainty avoidance are comfortable with situations that are ambiguous. There are many cultures in between as well.[477] Hofstede believes based on his research that "on the national cultural level, tendencies toward prejudices, rigidity and dogmatism, intolerance of different opinions, traditionalism, superstition, racism, and ethnocentrism" are all related to the intolerance of ambiguity.[478]

These countries are listed as having high uncertainty avoidance: Russia,** China,** Portugal, Japan, Peru, France, Argentina, Mexico,* Colombia, Brazil, Pakistan, Taiwan, Germany,* Austria, Italy, Venezuela, Israel, Turkey, Chile, Spain, Yugoslavia, Belgium, and Greece.[479]

These countries are listed as having low uncertainty avoidance: Iran, Switzerland, Australia, South Africa, Canada, Philippines, Sweden, Denmark,

---

[470] Lane, 72.
[471] Lane, 73.
[472] Lane, 73.
[473] Lane, 79.
[474] Hofstede, 29.
[475] Hofstede, 146.
[476] Lane, 79.
[477] Lane, 79.
[478] Hofstede, 146.
[479] Lane, 83. Lane referenced Hofstede, 315. *These country categories changed during further research conducted by Fernandez,. Carlson, Stepina, and Nicholson in "Hofstede's Country Classification 25 Years Later," *Journal of Social Psychology* 137: 1 (1997), 43. **These countries were added in more recent research.

Singapore, Hong Kong, Great Britain, India, United States,* New Zealand, Norway, Netherlands, Finland, and Thailand.[480]

Another aspect of the authority dimension is power distance.[481] Power distance deals with the comfort the people feel about unequal distribution of power. A large power distance means the people are comfortable with having a large distance between themselves and the people who have power over them.[482] Hofstede observes power distance provides "different solutions to the basic problem of human inequality," such as "prestige, wealth, and power."[483] In cultures with a large power distance, people are fine with having authority (supervisor, politician) tell them what to do without their input.[484] In cultures with small power distance, the people have low tolerance for unequal distribution of power and are not comfortable when there is limited access to power.[485]

These countries are listed as having large power distance: China,** Philippines, Mexico, Yugoslavia, Brazil, France, Turkey, Thailand, Portugal, Greece, Iran, Pakistan, Japan,* Spain, Taiwan, Chile,* Peru, Belgium, Colombia, Hong Kong, Singapore, India, Venezuela,* Russia.**[486]

These countries are listed as having small power distance: South Africa, United States, Netherlands, Germany, Switzerland, Sweden, Ireland, Denmark, Austria, Israel, New Zealand, Norway, Finland, Great Britain, Australia, Canada, Argentina, Italy.[487]

Relationship

In the relationship dimension, there are collective cultures and individualistic cultures. Hofstede sees this "is related to the integration of individuals into primary groups."[488] He writes, "In some cultures, individualism

---

[480] Lane, 83. Lane referenced Hofstede, 315. *These country categories changed during further research conducted by Fernandez, Carlson, Stepina, and Nicholson in "Hofstede's Country Classification 25 Years Later," *Journal of Social Psychology* 137: 1 (1997), 43. **These countries were added in more recent research.

[481] Lane, 80.

[482] Lane, 80.

[483] Hofstede, 29, 79.

[484] Lane80.

[485] Lane, 80-81.

[486] Lane, 84. Lane referenced Hofstede, 315. *These country categories changed during further research conducted by Fernandez, Carlson, Stepina, and Nicholson in "Hofstede's Country Classification 25 Years Later," *Journal of Social Psychology* 137:1 (1997), 43. **These countries were added in more recent research.

[487] Lane, 84. Lane referenced Hofstede, 315. *These country categories changed during further research conducted by Fernandez, Carlson, Stepina, and Nicholson in "Hofstede's Country Classification 25 Years Later," *Journal of Social Psychology* 137:1 (1997), 43. **These countries were added in more recent research.

[488] Hofstede, 29.

is seen as a blessing and a source of well-being; in others, it is seen as alienating."[489] People in collective cultures see themselves as part of a group, such as their family, tribe, or community. They see themselves relating to others as part of a group, instead of relating to others as unique individuals. For example, the Korean culture is a collective culture.[490]

In individualistic cultures, people relate to others on a one-on-one basis. They see themselves as individuals, separate from family or community. The United States is an individualistic culture, as are many low context cultures.[491]

In collective cultures, the issue of "face" or honor is very important. The people in these cultures would fear "losing face" or feeling shame or losing honor. It guides how people in these cultures interact with each other. The principles based on honor and avoiding shame will determine the appropriate behavior and how decisions are made.[492]

Lane observes that the relationship dimension can "also be referred to as the identity dimension because these beliefs not only form the basis for relationships with others but also the basis for how we view ourselves."[493]

These countries are listed as having individual cultures: United States, Great Britain, Canada, Italy, Denmark, France, Norway, Germany, Finland, Israel, Spain, Austria, South Africa, Switzerland, Ireland, Sweden, Belgium, New Zealand, Netherlands, Australia.[494]

These countries are listed as having collective cultures: India, Argentina, Brazil, Greece, Mexico,* Portugal, Chile,* Singapore, Peru, Colombia, Taiwan.[495]

Time

Cultures have different ways of looking at time. Hofstede notes this is "related to the choice of focus for people's efforts: the future or the present."[496] Some cultures such as the United States, Canada, and Western European countries see time as "limited" and "evolving."[497] However, most of the rest of

---

[489] Hofstede, 209.

[490] Lane, 86.

[491] Lane, 87.

[492] Lane, 88-89.

[493] Lane, 86.

[494] Lane, 96. Lane referenced Hofstede, 315. *These country categories changed during further research conducted by Fernandez, Carlson, Stepina, and Nicholson in "Hofstede's Country Classification 25 Years Later," *Journal of Social Psychology* 137:1 (1997), 43. **These countries were added in more recent research.

[495] Lane, 96. Lane referenced Hofstede, 315. *These country categories changed during further research conducted by Fernandez, Carlson, Stepina, and Nicholson in "Hofstede's Country Classification 25 Years Later," *Journal of Social Psychology* 137:1 (1997), 43. **These countries were added in more recent research.

[496] Hofstede, 29.

[497] Lane, 98.

the world sees time as abundant and historical.[498] Punctuality and "effective" use of time would be important for cultures that see time as limited. It can also lead to conflicts with people whose culture sees time as abundant.

Based on the Chinese Value Survey (CVS), an instrument developed by Michael Harris Bond in Hong Kong from values suggested by Chinese scholars, here is the ranking of 23 countries in Long-Term Orientation (choice of focus for people's efforts for the future rather than the present): 1) China, 2) Hong Kong, 3) Taiwan, 4) Japan, 5) South Korea, 6) Brazil, 7) India, 8) Thailand, 9) Singapore, 10) Netherlands, 11) Bangladesh, 12) Sweden, 13) Poland, 14) Germany (F.R.), 15) Australia, 16) New Zealand, 17) United States, 18) Great Britain, 19) Zimbabwe, 20) Canada, 21) Philippines, 22) Nigeria, 23) Pakistan.[499]

Worldview

Worldview is defined as the "culturally agreed upon perception of reality, in other words, worldview bridges the gap between objective reality and a person's perception of it."[500] Kraft perceives that every cultural entity has a worldview. A cultural entity can be "a culture, subculture, academic discipline, social class, religious, political, or economic organization, or any similar grouping with a distinct value system."[501]

Currently, there are three categories of the way people think – premodern, modern, and postmodern.[502] Another category may be "anti-modern."[503] Some culture's worldview can let them accept a faith system easier than another worldview. For example, Lane writes that "premodern and postmodern thinkers accept spiritual realities more easily than modern thinkers."[504]

For the premodern thinkers, truth is subjective, knowledge is mystical (capricious), perspective is holistic, and evidence is experiential (group then individual). For modern thinkers, truth is objective, knowledge is scientific, perspective is dualistic, linear, and evidence is empirical. For postmodern thinkers, truth is subjective (experience), knowledge is mystical (understandable), perspective is holistic, and evidence is experiential (individual then group).[505]

By understanding how different people think, we will not be surprised when we find that their way of thinking or even logic is different from ours, especially

---

[498] Lane, 98-99.
[499] Hofstede, 29.
[500] Lane, 106. Referenced Darrell Whiteman, "Culture, Values, and Worldviews: Anthropology for Mission Practice" (lecture given at Overseas Ministries Study Center in New Haven, Connecticut, January 1999).
[501] Kraft, 43.
[502] Lane, 106.
[503] Lane, 201.
[504] Lane, 107.
[505] Lane, 107.

when it comes to spiritual things. We can then try to think of the issue from their perspective or with their way of thinking.

In the Western worldview, people "see objects in isolation and place these objects in categories."[506] For Western worldview thinkers, reality is defined by rules that describe the relationship between objects.[507] In the Eastern worldview, people "see relationships—including relationships with nature—at the heart of reality."[508] For the Eastern worldview thinkers, there "are rules about how to live harmoniously in those relationships, but nothing can be completely controlled."[509] Another characteristic of Eastern worldview thinkers is that history affects them much more than Western worldview thinkers.[510]

Nisbett states that "in general the farther West one goes from East Asia, the more individualistic thinking becomes. Some of the characteristics of Eastern thought also hold true for many other collectivist societies, such as those in Africa and minority subcultures in the West."[511]

Honor and Shame

The website honorshame.com states that "honor-shame is the primary OS for 80% of the world."[512]

The website lists these five keys for relationships in honor-shame cultures:[513] 1) Give gifts, 2) Know roles, 3) Don't expose, 4) Be clean, and 5) Guest well.[514]

The honorshame.com website states that for honor-shame cultures giving gifts is important because it is "structured around reciprocity – everybody must be sharing and gifting with one another."[515] Since honor-shame cultures tend to be hierarchical, we should also dress, relate, eat, and communicate according to our place in the hierarchy.[516] We need to avoid shaming someone in an honor-shame culture because shame can cause people to "become resistant and

---

[506] Katie J. Rawson, *Crossing Cultures with Jesus: Sharing Good News with Sensitivity and Grace,* (Downers Grove, IL: InterVarsity, 2015), 82. Rawson cited Richard E. Nisbett, *The Geography of Thought: How Asians and Westerners Think Differently...and Why,* (New York: Simon & Schuster: Free Press, 2003), 10.

[507] Rawson, 82. Rawson cited Nisbett, 10.

[508] Rawson, 82-83. Rawson cited Nisbett, 45.

[509] Rawson, 82-83. Rawson cited Nisbett, 45.

[510] Rawson, 82-83. Rawson cited Nisbett, 45.

[511] Rawson, 83.

[512] HonorShame, "About HonorShame.com," <http://honorshame.com/about> (2/28/2017).

[513] HonorShame, "5 Keys for Relationships in HonorShame Contexts," <http://honorshame.com/5-keys-for-relationships-in-honorshame-contexts/> (2/28/2017).

[514] HonorShame.

[515] HonorShame.

[516] HonorShame.

defensive."[517] It is also important to follow "purity rules" such as how we dress in an honor-shame culture.[518] We need to be a good guest in honor-shame cultures because they "are typically very proud of their hospitality," which "often means allowing yourself to be served" and giving "effusive thanks and compliments" after the meal.[519]

In *Crossing Cultures with Jesus*, Katie Rawson points to the guilt, shame, and fear experienced by humans due to the Fall. She writes, "Roland Muller, a longtime tentmaker missionary in the Middle East, observes that after their disobedience, Adam and Eve experienced guilt, shame, and fear in place of the innocence, honor, and power they had known beforehand."[520] Muller sees three lenses with which people tend to view the world: innocence-guilt, honor-shame, or power-fear.[521] Benjamin Hegeman, a missiologist and former missionary to Benin, West Africa, adds a fourth lens: joy-pain.[522] Hegeman supports his view from Revelation 15:3-4, the Song of Moses and the Lamb. These verses ascribe to the Lamb "marvelous deeds (power), just and true ways (innocence and integrity), glory (honor), and worship from all nations (joy)."[523]

Rawson observes that joy and pain are not included in many recent value systems, but she includes them because "of the many references to them in the Scriptures and because they resonate strongly with younger generations worldwide."[524]

Rawson explains that "*Innocence* is a sense of integrity, justice, and righteousness" and in societies that value innocence like the U.S., people are motivated to obey the law and to avoid a guilty conscience.[525] Rawson explains honor as "glory, respect, and a good reputation" and shame or disgrace as "a sense of being deeply flawed or having lost honor in a moral sense."[526]

Rawson writes that in "societies where honor is the leading value (e.g., most East Asian and Middle Eastern societies), people are motivated to increase or protect the honor of the group or self and avoid shame in the eyes of others or in their own eyes."[527] In honor-led societies, people would try to save face for others, themselves, or the group.[528]

---

[517] HonorShame.

[518] HonorShame.

[519] HonorShame.

[520] Roland Muller, *Honor and Shame: Unlocking the Door*, (Bloomington, IN: Xlibris Corp, 2000), 19. Cited in Katie Rawson *Crossing Cultures*, 92.

[521] Muller, 92.

[522] Benjamin Hegeman, "The Flight of the Swans: Discerning Hidden Values in Global cultures," *Evangelical Missions Quarterly* 46:2 (April 2010), 166-7. Referenced in Katie Rawson 92.

[523] Hegeman, 168. Referenced in Katie Rawson, 92.

[524] Rawson, 93.

[525] Rawson, 93.

[526] Rawson, 93.

[527] Rawson, 93.

[528] Rawson, 93.

Rawson describes power as "the ability to rule self and others, win battles, and obtain success or good luck" and weakness or fear as a "sense of powerlessness or slavery in the presence of evil powers, including spiritual (evil spirits), domestic (abusers), or political powers."[529] Rawson writes, that in "societies dominated by power (totalitarian and tribal), people are motivated by the desire for power and fear of government authorities, spirits, or ancestors."[530]

Rawson explains joy as "delight, pleasure and adventure" and pain or futility as "a sense of emotional or physical distress or yearning for an unattainable joy."[531] People in joy-pain dominated societies such as France would be motivated to seek joy or pleasure and avoid pain.[532]

Rawson defines shame as being "flawed, impure, or defiled"[533] and face as "the objective moral and social reality of honor."[534] Rawson sees the new fame-shame culture of the younger generation is "an individualist form of honor-shame in which people vie for public approval through social media and there is less or no thought about saving the face of others."[535]

Rawson listed the following distribution of values:[536]

1. North America, Northern Europe, Australia, New Zealand – Primary Value: Innocence-Guilt. Secondary Value: Honor-Shame (Southern and small-town US), Fame-Shame (postmodern).
2. Asia, Middle East, Africa, Latin America, most Old Testament societies – Primary Value: Honor-Shame. Secondary Value: Power-Weakness (fear).
3. China, tribal societies, South Asia – Primary Value: Power-Weakness (fear). Secondary Value: Honor-Shame.
4. France, some members of younger generations worldwide – Primary Value: Joy (pleasure)-Pain. Secondary Value: Innocence-Guilt, Honor-Shame.
5. Asian American immigrants, Southern Europe Roman society in the New Testament – Primary Value: Honor-Shame. Secondary Value: Innocence-Guilt.[537]

---

[529] Rawson, 93.
[530] Rawson, 93.
[531] Rawson, 93.
[532] Rawson, 93.
[533] Rawson, 96.
[534] Rawson, 97. Rawson cites Christopher L. Flanders, "Face," in William A. Dyrness and Veli-Matti Kärkkäinen, eds., *Global Dictionary of Theology*, (Downers Grove, IL: IVP Academic, 2008), 308-9.
[535] Rawson, 95. Rawson cites Andy Crouch, "The Return of Shame," *Christianity Today* 59:2 (2015), 32-41.
[536] Rawson, 95.
[537] Rawson, 95.

Cultural Values

In *Multicultural Management*, Elashmawi and Harris reported the following top five priority of values by country:[538]

-Japan: Relationships, Group harmony, Family, Freedom, Cooperation
-Korean: Family, Cooperation, Relationships, Group harmony, Spirituality
-Indonesian: Relationships, Family, Reputation, Cooperation, Group harmony
-Malaysian: Family, Group harmony, Cooperation, Relationships, Spirituality
-Filipino: Family, Spirituality, Reputation, Cooperation, Freedom
-Thai: Seniority, Reputation, Relationships, Cooperation, Authority
-Chinese: Equality, Freedom, Family security, Group harmony, Cooperation
-Taiwanese: Competition, Family security, Reputation, Seniority, Authority
-Hong Kong: Competition, Relationships, Reputation, Time, Possessions
-Singaporean: Relationships, Family security, Openness, Cooperation, Freedom
-Arab: Seniority, Spirituality, Reputation, Family, Authority.

From this research, we see three Asian countries (Japan, Indonesian, Singaporean) value relationships most. Three Asian countries (Korean, Malaysian, Filipino) value family most. Two Asian countries (Taiwanese, Hong Kong) value competition most. Thai and Arab value seniority most. Chinese value equality most.

Elashmawi and Harris also reported differences in values between the traditional and new generation. In the new generation of Japanese, the top five cultural values are: Freedom, Relationships, Family, Equality, and Self-reliance.[539] For the new generation of Thais, the top five cultural values are: Reputation, Family security, Relationships, Cooperation, and Self-reliance.[540] We see that cultural values are not static and can change with new generations.

For Americans, the top 20 values are: 1) Freedom, 2) Independence, 3) Self-reliance, 4) Equality, 5) Individualism, 6) Competition, 7) Efficiency, 8) Time, 9) Directness, 10) Openness, 11) Aggressiveness, 12) Informality, 13) Future-orientation, 14) Risk-taking, 15) Creativity, 16) Self-accomplishment, 17) Winning, 18) Money, 19) Material possessions, 20) Privacy.[541]

For the Japanese, the top 20 values are: 1) Belonging, 2) Group harmony, 3) Collectiveness, 4) Age/seniority, 5) Group consensus, 6) Cooperation, 7) Quality, 8) Patience, 9) Indirectness, 10) Go-between, 11) Interpersonal, 12) Hierarchy,

---

[538] Farid Elashmawi and Philip R. Harris, *Multicultural Management 2000: Essential Cultural Insights for Global Business Success*, (Houston, TX: Gulf Publishing Company, 1998), 68-69.
[539] Elashmawi and Harris, 71.
[540] Elashmawi and Harris, 71.
[541] Elashmawi and Harris, 72.

13) Continuation, 14) Conservative, 15) Information, 16) Group achievement, 17) Success, 18) Relationship, 19) Harmony with nature, 20) Networking.[542]

For the Arabs, the top 20 values are: 1) Family security, 2) Family harmony, 3) Parental guidance, 4) Age, 5) Authority, 6) Compromise, 7) Devotion, 8) Very patient, 9) Indirectness, 10) Hospitality, 11) Friendship, 12) Formal/admiration, 13) Past and present, 14) Religious belief, 15) Tradition, 16) Social recognition, 17) Reputation, 18) Friendship, 19) Belonging, 20) Family network.[543]

Lane notes that differing cultural values can create tensions. She writes, "If my highest value is self-reliance and I am working with someone who does not highly value that, then my efforts to safeguard that priority may be misunderstood."[544]

Building Relationships Cross-culturally

Lane believes the key to building relationships cross-culturally is to understand our own cultural lenses and the lenses of others because "each culture has a unique way of seeing life and relationships."[545] We also need to deal with the ethnocentrism and xenophobia in our hearts. Xenophobia refers to the fear of another culture. Xenophobia can have many causes and may lead to racism, hate groups, and crimes.[546] Ethnocentrism is the belief that one's own culture, race, or ethnicity is the best.[547] This is different from feeling good about who you are, it is about feeling superior to people of other cultures.[548] This can include being patronizing or stereotyping other cultures. It can also be seen when we invite others to be a part of our culture, and we do not let them be involved in a meaningful way, by treating them as "tokens." Ethnocentrism can also lead to intolerance toward people of other cultures.[549] Lane believes that we can respond either with xenophobia, ethnocentrism, or segregationism ("wanting cultures to coexist separately"), accepting ("wanting others to become like us"), or celebrating ("learning from and enjoying the diversity of others").[550] She writes, "If we choose to celebrate the diversity God has created, the possibilities for His kingdom are great."[551]

---

[542] Elashmawi and Harris, 72.
[543] Elashmawi and Harris, 72.
[544] Lane, 122.
[545] Lane, 47.
[546] Lane, 37.
[547] Lane, 38.
[548] Lane, 38.
[549] Lane, 38.
[550] Lane, 171.
[551] Lane, 171.

Lane points to the scriptures to be generous and hospitable such as 2 Corinthians 9:6-8, Romans 12:13, 1 Timothy 6:18, and Hebrews 13:16 to show how and why we should build relationships cross-culturally.[552]

Lane sees tremendous opportunity in the U.S. for developing relationships with neighbors who have come from other cultures and countries. She writes, "The United States has the ability to provide a new home for millions of people who have come here for a multitude of reasons. While they may not have in mind finding a relationship with God through Jesus that might well be the greatest opportunity they receive in this country if we are willing to reach out beyond our cultural comfort zone."[553]

Lane lists ways to develop cross-cultural relationships.[554] The following is a summary of the "attitude," "aptitude," "affinities," and "actions" needed in cross-cultural relationships. First, the person's "attitude" should be that of a humble learner who sees God in the relationship, focuses on the relationship, and does not think his/her own culture is the best or attempt to prove it.[555] Second, the person should have the "aptitude" that understands the culture lenses, knows his/her own culture and other cultures, and learns observational skills and right ways of dealing with cross-cultural conflicts.[556] Third, there should be "affinities" that look for common interests in cross-cultural relationships, discover projects to work with other culture groups, and be emotionally connected with people and families from other culture groups.[557] Finally, there should be "actions" such as taking initiative though not being too direct, showing interest and trusting God, enjoying a meal together and sharing his/her own culture, asking questions and being flexible, and praying and observing the behaviors of the people in the other culture.[558]

Things to Consider in Intercultural Relations

The following are from John W. Berry, who listed these dimensions of cultural variation that are important in intercultural relations:[559]

1. Diversity – "How many different positions, roles, and institutions are there? Are there other variations within culture (e.g., regional, ethnic)?"[560]

---

[552] Lane, 143.
[553] Lane, 171.
[554] Lane, 172.
[555] Lane, 172.
[556] Lane, 172.
[557] Lane, 172.
[558] Lane, 172.
[559] John W. Berry, "Fundamental Psychological Processes in Intercultural Relations," in Dan Landis, Janet M. Bennett, and Milton J. Bennett, eds., *Handbook of Intercultural Training*, (Thousand Oaks, CA: Sage Publications, 2004), 170.
[560] Berry, in Landis, Bennett, and Bennett, eds., 170.

2. Equality – "Are these differences arranged in horizontal (egalitarian) or vertical (hierarchical) social structures?"[561]
3. Conformity – "How tightly structured are the various parts? How much are individuals enmeshed in the social order?"[562]
4. Wealth – "What is the average level of wealth (gross domestic product per person) available to support the necessities of life?"[563]
5. Space – "How do individuals use space during interpersonal relationships? Are eye and body contact frequent?"[564]
6. Time – "Are people concerned about promptness and schedules? Do they engage each other one-on-one or have multiple interactions at one time?"[565]

Five Thresholds in Cross-cultural Evangelism

Katie Rawson lists five thresholds in cross-cultural evangelism (she credits this to Sarah Akutagawa): 1) Distrust to Trust, 2) Apathy to Curiosity, 3) Curiosity to Openness, 4) Openness to Seeking, and 5) Entering the Kingdom.[566]

Rawson perceives that the "five thresholds play out differently in each cultural context because the reasons for distrust and cultural strongholds to be overcome are different."[567] She sees the importance of inviting each individual to trust the entire campus fellowship or small group. Rawson writes, "These groups need to build trust with the communities of the individuals they attract, asking about and caring for family and friends near and far."[568]

How to Move from Ethnocentrism[569]

Milton J. Bennett, in the chapter "Towards Ethnorelativism: A Developmental Model of Intercultural Sensitivity," sees that intercultural communication training and education is to help change our "natural" behavior to develop our intercultural sensitivity.[570] He writes, "With the concepts and skills developed in

---

561 Berry, in Landis, Bennett, and Bennett, eds., 170.
562 Berry, in Landis, Bennett, and Bennett, eds., 170.
563 Berry, in Landis, Bennett, and Bennett, eds., 170.
564 Berry, in Landis, Bennett, and Bennett, eds., 170.
565 Berry, in Landis, Bennett, and Bennett, eds., 170.
566 Rawson, 129.
567 Rawson, 128.
568 Rawson, 128.
569 Enoch Wan, "Ethnocentrism," in A. Scott Moreau, ed., *Evangelical Dictionary of World Missions*, (Baker Books, 2005), 324-325.
570 Milton J. Bennett, "Towards Ethnorelativism: A Developmental Model of Intercultural Sensitivity," in *Education for the Intercultural Experience*, R. Michael Paige, ed., (Yarmouth, ME: Intercultural Press, Inc., 1993), 21.

this field, we ask learners to transcend traditional ethnocentrism and to explore new relationships across cultural boundaries."[571]

The following is "A Developmental Model of Intercultural Sensitivity" from Bennett:[572]

The Ethnocentric Stages
I.   DENIAL
     A. Isolation
     B. Separation
II.   DEFENSE
     A. Denigration
     B. Superiority
     C. Reversal
III.   MINIMIZATION
     A. Physical Universalism
     B. Transcendent Universalism
The Ethnorelative Stages
IV.   ACCEPTANCE
     A. Respect for Behavioral Difference
     B. Respect for Value Difference
V.   ADAPTATION
     A. Empathy
     B. Pluralism
VI.   INTEGRATION
     A. Contextual Evaluation
     B. Constructive Marginality

Handling Cross-Cultural Conflicts

In *Cross-cultural Conflict: Building Relationships for Effective Ministry*, Duane Elmer shared the principles to try to change a situation in a foreign land. It is derived from an experience of a missionary who wanted to convince the local people, especially the traditional healer, to use disinfectants for their eye infections. We can learn from these principles when trying to bring change to the lives of those with whom we are developing cross-cultural relationships. Elmer suggests principles such as choosing friendship over confrontation, using local ceremony, technology and personnel to implement the change, introducing change that does not violate the patterns and roles of people involved and not exalting oneself, building on what the people already know and practice, making

---

[571] Bennett, in Paige, ed., 21.
[572] Bennett, in Paige, ed., 29.

sure the change is not dependent on the outsiders being there, and keeping central the role of the Holy Spirit.[573]

Elmer lists the following "Principles for Cross-Cultural Conflict Resolution":[574]

1. The degree to which shame, face, and honor are core cultural values will determine how important it is to choose an indirect method.
2. If the other person has had extensive exposure to Western culture, sensitive directness may be acceptable, understood, and not offensive.
3. All forms of confrontation should occur in private, if possible, so as to minimize any loss of face.
4. Familiarize yourself with the stories, parables, fables, legends, and heroes of a culture in order to appropriately interpret their use in conflict situations.
5. Understand the various indirect methods used in the Two-Thirds World and be alert to which ones are used and under what circumstances.
6. Build a close relationship with a host-country person who will be able to help you interpret confusing situations.
7. Ask God for help in understanding and applying unfamiliar conflict resolution strategies.
8. Scripture is the final judge of all cultural forms; prayer and discussion may be required before some cultural expressions are embraced.

Sherwood G. Lingenfelter and Marvin K. Mayers, in *Ministering Cross-culturally: A Model for Effective Personal Relationships,* listed the following cross-cultural tensions that may occur:[575] tensions about time (time or event-orientation),[576] tensions regarding judgment (dichotomistic or holistic),[577] tensions associated with handling crises (crisis or non-crisis orientation),[578] tensions over goals (task or person orientation),[579] tensions about self-worth (status or achievement focus, prestige is ascribed or acquired),[580] and tensions regarding vulnerability (concealment or willingness to expose vulnerability).[581] The authors see that the key to doing effective ministry in any culture is to learn to adapt to it. We need to compare our cultural orientation to the other culture

---

[573] Duane Elmer, *Cross-cultural Conflict: Building Relationships for Effective Ministry,* (Downers Grove, IL: InterVarsity Press, 1993), 61.
[574] Elmer, 181.
[575] Sherwood G. Lingenfelter and Marvin K. Mayers, *Ministering Cross-culturally: An Incarnational Model for Personal Relationships,* 3rd ed. (Grand Rapids, MI: Baker Academic, 2016), vii.
[576] Lingenfelter and Mayers, 29.
[577] Lingenfelter and Mayers, 42.
[578] Lingenfelter and Mayers, 58.
[579] Lingenfelter and Mayers, 69.
[580] Lingenfelter and Mayers, 85.
[581] Lingenfelter and Mayers, 95.

and "identify areas in our value orientation in which we must adapt and change to be effective in our ministry."[582]

The Chinese Culture from Others' Perspective

To interact with other cultures, we need to also understand our own culture from the perspectives of others. *Encountering the Chinese: A Guide for Americans* is written for Americans to understand Chinese culture. It is useful to understand how to explain our culture to people in another culture. Wenzhong and Grove list the three fundamental values of the Chinese as collectivism, large power distance, and intragroup harmony.[583] Wenzhong and Grove note that in China's large cities, where Western influence is especially strong, the Chinese are becoming less collectivistic. This can be seen in the frequency of job-hopping of Chinese employees among Western businesses.[584]

Wenzhong and Grove note that another change is that the emphasis on socialist egalitarianism over the past thirty or forty years in the PRC has eroded the Confucian way of thinking, such as the "respect for age, seniority, rank, maleness, and family background."[585]

Seniority is still very important in Chinese society. In Chinese, there are no age-neutral words for brother or sister. Age is also important in community affairs. "What an older person says generally carries more weight in the meetings of the neighborhood committee than the opinions of younger people."[586] Younger people are to be deferential to those older to them.[587]

However, the maintaining of harmonious relationships with family members, close friends, and colleagues, and other primary group members is still very important for Chinese people.[588]

Cross-cultural Communication

David J. Hesselgrave, in *Communicating Christ Cross-Culturally: An Introduction to Missionary Communication,* discusses how Christians should communicate Christ cross-culturally because of Christ's command to disciple

---

[582] Lingenfelter and Mayers, 110.
[583] Hu Wenzhong and Cornelius L. Grove, *Encountering the Chinese: A Guide for Americans,* (Yarmouth, ME: Intercultural Press, Inc., 1999), 5-8.
[584] Wenzhong and Grove, 7.
[585] Wenzhong and Grove, 7.
[586] Wenzhong and Grove, 7.
[587] Wenzhong and Grove, 7.
[588] Wenzhong and Grove, 8.

the nations.[589] The responsibility to understand culture and initiating the process of contextualization is, from Hesselgrave's perspective, with the missionaries who have the task to deliver the Christian message across cultural boundaries. Hesselgrave writes, "This means that the missionary needs to learn to communicate Christ to respondents in terms of their (the respondents') way of viewing the world, their way of thinking, their way of expressing themselves in language, their way of acting, their response to media, their way of interacting, and their way of deciding future courses of action."[590]

Hesselgrave lists the following seven dimensions of cross-cultural communication: 1) Worldviews – ways of perceiving the world, 2) Cognitive Processes – ways of thinking, 3) Linguistic Forms – ways of expressing ideas, 4) Behavioral Patterns – ways of acting, 5) Social Structures – ways of interacting, 6) Media Influence – ways of channeling the message, and 7) Motivational Resources – ways of deciding.[591]

To understand these seven dimensions of another culture is not an easy task; this requires investments of time and energy. Therefore, cross-cultural communication of Christ is a process of learning about another person, their culture, and how God wants us to communicate the gospel to them.

Ajith Fernando, in *Sharing the Truth in Love: How to Relate to People of Other Faiths*, urges respect and humility towards people of other faiths. We should have joyous enthusiasm, not arrogance when serving them, with an attitude of humble servanthood.[592] Fernando also relates the importance of sensitivity to others, getting to know other faiths, and biblical spirituality in his book.[593]

Mentoring Background

Mentoring, throughout history, has been the way people have passed experience and values from one generation to the next. It can be said to be as old as civilization itself.[594] In the Bible, we see mentoring examples such as Eli and Samuel, Elijah and Elisha, Moses and Joshua, Barnabas and Paul, and Paul and Timothy. Stanley and Clinton write, "Throughout human history, mentoring was the primary means of passing on knowledge and skills in every field – from Greek philosophers to sailors – and in every culture."[595]

---

[589] Hesselgrave, 31.
[590] Hesselgrave, 163-164.
[591] Hesselgrave, 164.
[592] Ajith Fernando, *Sharing the Truth in Love: How to Relate to People of Other Faiths*, (Grand Rapids, MI: Discovery House Publishers, 2001), 51-52.
[593] Fernando, Table of Contents.
[594] Paul D. Stanley and J. Robert Clinton, *Connecting: The Mentoring Relationships You Need to Succeed in Life*, (Colorado Springs, CO: Navpress, 1992), 17.
[595] Stanley and Clinton, 17.

However, in the modern age, learning has shifted to rely on computers, classrooms, books, and videos. Thus, the relational connection between the knowledge-and-experience giver and the receiver has weakened or is nonexistent.[596]

Stanley and Clinton see the common stories in mentoring usually start with someone in need who meets someone further along in experience and can contribute to that need. As the relationship is established, the more experienced person shares from his/her experience and learning to help the person in need, and through the sharing the mentor passes to the mentee "the power to grow through a situation," which is called "empowerment."[597]

The heart of mentoring is the process of "empowerment" in a mentoring relationship.[598] Thus, mentoring can be defined as "a relational experience in which one person empowers another by sharing God-given resources."[599] The God-given resources can include wisdom, experiences, patterns, habits of obedience, principles, and other elements.[600]

Stanley and Clinton discuss features of mentoring relationships such as the mentor and mentee sharing perspectives on different situations that they encounter, having regular meetings whether it's weekly, bi-weekly or monthly, and initiating the mentoring relationship from either person.[601]

Here is a more detailed definition of mentoring from Stanley and Clinton: "Mentoring is a relational process in which a mentor, who knows or has experienced something, transfers that something (resources of wisdom, information, experience, confidence, insight, relationships, status, etc.) to a mentee, at an appropriate time and manner, so that it facilitates development or empowerment."[602]

Stanley and Clinton define seven mentoring types/functions:[603]

-Intensive mentoring: 1) Discipler, 2) Spiritual Guide, 3) Coach
-Occasional mentoring: 4) Counselor, 5) Teacher, 6) Sponsor
-Passive mentoring: 7) Model – Contemporary and Historical.

Stanley and Clinton see three dynamics are vital in a mentoring relationship: attraction, responsiveness, and accountability. In attraction, the mentor possesses "perspective, certain skills, experience, values and commitments modeled, perceived wisdom, position, character, knowledge, and influence" that the mentee is looking for and as the attraction grows, the trust and confidence

---

[596] Stanley and Clinton, 17-18.
[597] Stanley and Clinton, 32.
[598] Stanley and Clinton, 32.
[599] Stanley and Clinton, 33.
[600] Stanley and Clinton, 33.
[601] Stanley and Clinton, 33.
[602] Stanley and Clinton, 40.
[603] Stanley and Clinton, 42.

in the mentor will help strengthen the relationship and help the mentee be empowered.[604] In responsiveness, the mentee should have a teachable spirit so the empowerment may be quickened and enhanced.[605] In accountability, there should be "periodic reviews and evaluation" from the mentor.[606]

Mentoring is seen as primarily a relationship between two people, in which one person shares valuable elements with the other person in order for change or empowerment to take place in the mentee. It is important that the definition of what is shared is God-given resources. Thus, it is referring to spiritual/biblical things that are passed from one person to another. The relationship is made to fulfill God's purpose and for God's glory. There are different types of mentors. To fulfill God's mission, we need all different types of mentors. In this modern age, there are many mentoring avenues. There are resources from books, the internet, learning over distance, relationships over distance, and people we can find through different communication and church community channels. We also need to be aware of the dynamics in mentoring. If we want to be a mentor, are we developing and gaining the skills, knowledge, and experience that people need in mentoring? If we want to find mentors, are we the kind of person with the attitude and potential such that others would want to invest their time to mentor us?

Cross-cultural Leadership

Cross-cultural leadership and discipleship is at the heart of missionary work.[607] James E. Plueddemann perceives missions as "the cross-cultural task of making disciples of Jesus." The tasks of mission include evangelism, church planting, discipleship, theological education, leadership development, and partnership in world missions.[608]

How can we adapt to different cultures as we serve cross-culturally? By honoring and submitting to one another in love. Plueddemann writes, "All of us in the body of Christ, no matter what our formal position, must love and obey the Lord while we honor and submit to one another in love. If we follow this principle, we can adapt to different cultural values in the way we lead and the way we follow."[609]

Plueddmann sees an effective leader in cross-cultural situations "will be flexible in their style by assessing the *cultural* expectations of leaders and

---

[604] Stanley and Clinton, 43.
[605] Stanley and Clinton, 43.
[606] Stanley and Clinton, 43-44.
[607] James E. Plueddemann, *Leading Across Cultures: Effective Ministry and Mission in the Global Church,* (Downers Grove, IL: InterVarsity Press, 2009), 59.
[608] Plueddemann, 47.
[609] Plueddemann, 108.

followers."[610] They will change their leadership style as the cultural situation changes. They will adapt themselves to different understanding and expectations as they work or serve under leaders with different cultural backgrounds. In summary, "Both leaders and followers must be aware of the expectations of the host culture, adapting accordingly."[611]

Plueddemann defines good leaders as *"fervent disciples of Jesus Christ, gifted by the Holy Spirit, with a passion to bring glory to God. They use their gift of leadership by taking initiative to focus, harmonize, and enhance the gifts of others for the sake of developing people and cultivating the kingdom of God."*[612]

Cross-cultural leadership involves a willingness to be flexible and adapt to different cultural situations in order to fulfill the mission work. Cross-cultural leadership involves understanding the cultures of other people in order to lead or to follow them as one serves. It is important to know the expectations of the other culture in order to adapt accordingly. All of these facets must be practiced in evangelism, church planting, discipleship, theological education, leadership development, and partnership in world missions.

Suggestions to Contextualize Cross-cultural Ministries of Chinese Churches

We can contextualize cross-cultural ministries for Chinese diaspora based on their cultural traits and history. Listed below are 11 cultural traits and ideas to contextualize and mobilize the SFBA Chinese churches to minister cross-culturally to diaspora groups:

I.   Cultural Trait: Industrious (hardworking nature)

Chinese diaspora Christians can serve as encouragers and motivators of other diaspora groups through their experiences of working hard and succeeding in America. Co-author Lei went back to his junior high school to share with the mostly minority students in an algebra class on how he used algebra in his work as an engineer. He used the opportunity to motivate the students to see how their schoolwork will help them succeed in the future.

Ministry ideas:

1.   Offer seminars on surviving financially as immigrants.
2.   Offer seminars on parenting as immigrants.
3.   Offer seminars on investing in real estate and stocks as immigrants.

---

[610] Plueddemann, 153.
[611] Plueddemann, 153.
[612] Plueddemann, 171.

4. Allowing other diaspora Christian fellowship groups without building facility to use the church facility for their meetings.
5. Adopt newly arrived diaspora families to pray for and serve.
6. Provide resources and assistance to new diaspora Christian fellowships.
7. Adopt a diaspora group Christian fellowship to pray for and serve.
8. Visit diaspora families and churches to learn about their financial, parenting, and investments challenges, and pray for ways to serve them.
9. Partner with diaspora churches to jointly host conferences/seminars on financial, parenting, and investment topics.
10. Make friends with diaspora parents and share activities their children are involved in. For example, invite them to your children's birthday parties.

II.   Cultural Traits: Value education and social mobility

Chinese diaspora Christians who are faculty members can reach out to diaspora students to serve them. Successful Chinese diaspora Christians can share their experiences with other diaspora students.

Ministry ideas:

1. Organize activities for diaspora communities to connect with local police officers and local officials.
2. Show Chinese Christians how the early Chinese immigrants were ministered to by the American Christian workers in the areas of education, faith, and sex trafficking and how this should motivate the Chinese Christians to serve other diaspora groups in the same way.
3. Start anti-human trafficking ministries that seek to minister to the victims from diaspora groups.
4. Partner with diaspora groups to minister to victims of human trafficking locally and abroad.
5. Visit prisons and reach out to inmates who are from diaspora groups.
6. Visit aliens who are awaiting deportation.
7. Volunteer with organizations serving aliens.
8. Offer free/low cost legal service to aliens seeking legal status.
9. Offer free/low cost legal counsel to aliens for cases like traffic accidents, lawsuits, discrimination, and problems at work.
10. Offer free/low cost legal counsel to immigrants in abusive relationships.

III.   Cultural Trait: Confrontation avoidance (harmony)

Chinese diaspora Christians can serve as one of the mediators to bring together the different diaspora Christian groups, Caucasians, and African American groups. Chinese diaspora Christians can work for reconciliation between ethnic groups. They can also seek to bring healing to diaspora people who have been through traumatic experiences.

Ministry ideas:

1. Partner with other diaspora groups to host a reconciliation conference to help diaspora groups be reconciled to one another.
2. Actively reach out to diaspora groups which Chinese traditionally do not associate with to participate in joint activities and ministries.
3. Identify the refugee communities in the area and find ways to serve their physical, emotional, and spiritual needs.
4. Host conferences to bring the vision of diaspora ministries to the churches in the SFBA.
5. Start parachurch ministries to specifically minister to the diaspora groups, especially the unreached and unengaged groups.
6. Start a fellowship or network of church pastors/leaders who have a burden for diaspora ministries.
7. Host special camps for the children and youth of the diaspora groups to bring healing and restoration for those who have been through traumatic experiences.
8. Host charity concerts to benefit local refugees and needy diaspora groups.
9. Host healing and restoration conferences for diasporas from different regions that have experienced war and violence.
10. Identify ways to bring the gospel of peace to people of other religions.

IV.   Cultural Trait: Emphasis on relationship

Chinese diaspora Christians can extend their relational style to ministries to other diaspora groups by their hospitality, emphasis on relationships, and relational evangelism.

Ministry ideas:

1. Invite other diaspora groups to their homes and visit their homes and restaurants.
2. Make authentic Chinese food and invite diaspora groups during special festivals like Chinese New Year and August Moon Festival.
3. Attend the activities of other diaspora groups during their festivals.
4. Volunteer at community events that attract the various diaspora groups.

5. Develop relationship with other ethnic churches. Partner with other ethnic churches to serve the diaspora groups in the community. Invite their pastors to share about their ministries.
6. Start day care and after school programs that meet the needs of the children of diaspora groups.
7. Invite the youth of diaspora groups to sports activities with the youth from the churches.
8. Host field trips to various amusement parks or museums for children of diaspora groups.
9. Visit local ethnic restaurants and pray for God to open up opportunities to connect with them.
10. Start free English classes or classes that would appeal to recent immigrants. English classes are usually the first place to go for wives of overseas assignees.

V. Cultural Trait: High-context culture

Chinese diaspora Christians can use their experiences to share the gospel with other diaspora groups. They can share the gospel in contextual ways that the diaspora groups may find understandable and acceptable.

Ministry ideas:

1. Partner Chinese and other ethnic churches together to build a community center that would serve the needs of the immigrants in the community and include other ethnic groups in the leadership and staff of the community center. The center can offer free simple health services, translation help, counselors to help with immigration questions, family issues, and spiritual issues, classes specifically for women who stay at home while their husbands are working, and child-care facilities.
2. Start sports ministries that would interest the youth from diaspora groups and invite the youth from other churches to join.
3. Host summer camps for the children and youth of the diaspora groups.
4. Start day care and after school programs that meet the needs of the children of diaspora groups.
5. Identify elements in other religions of the diaspora groups that can allow Christians to present the gospel. Identify ways to explain the way of salvation by finding common elements or themes in other religions.
6. Find elements in Chinese culture that other diaspora groups like or admire, such as Chinese cooking and Chinese medicine, as ways to serve and to share the gospel.

7. Host gospel meetings that include Chinese performances such as traditional music, dance, or martial arts, and invite people from other diaspora groups to attend.
8. Use cultural exchange with other diaspora groups as ways to build relationships and share the gospel.
9. Identify common history or experiences with other diaspora groups to connect with them and to share the gospel.
10. Offer free/low cost Chinese language or martial arts classes to people from diaspora groups who may be interested.

VI.   Cultural Trait: Honor and shame

Chinese diaspora Christians can find ways to share the gospel with other diaspora groups that would avoid overtly shaming their hearers. They can find ways to share in a way that honors the people who are hearing the gospel.

Ministry ideas:

1. Partner with other Christian groups to outreach to the diaspora community through friendly, non-confrontational, and honoring methods of evangelism.
2. Offer confidential hotline for victims of marital abuse from diaspora groups.
3. Offer confidential hotline/service for people from diaspora groups seeking legal assistance.
4. Offer confidential hotline for diaspora people to inquire about Christianity in their languages.
5. Offer confidential shelters for people who need protection or temporary shelter.
6. Help local charity and government organizations to publicize their services to diaspora groups in a culturally sensitive and non-threatening way.
7. Serve as a confidential point of contact for people from diaspora groups to get help from local charity and government organizations.
8. Offer confidential and culturally sensitive counseling service to diaspora groups that respect their cultural structure.
9. Assist Christian counselors from diaspora groups with resources and contacts.
10. Support diaspora group Christians who want to go into counseling ministries with scholarships and resources.

VII.   Cultural Trait: Hybridization of lifestyle and cultural values

Chinese diaspora Christians can learn about other cultures and adapt their ministries and ways to share the gospel.

Ministry ideas:

1. Help build churches that are multi-ethnic and a hybrid of the different cultures.
2. Plant new churches that have a vision for diaspora ministries.
3. Create gospel material (tracts, magazines, books) that address the needs and culture of different people in the Bay area.
4. Create internet resources to connect people in the Bay area with churches and ministries.
5. Partner with other diaspora Christians to start fusion restaurants of different regional foods – such as a combination of Indian and Chinese. There may already be such restaurants. However, it would be a good witness to have Christians from different diaspora groups to partner together to create these new restaurants.
6. Create evangelistic ministries which train and equip diaspora Christians to reach out to people from other diasporas. For example, training Indian Christians to reach out to Chinese people, and vice versa.
7. Create gospel tracts with the multiple languages of people in the Bay area (i.e. Chinese, Vietnamese, Japanese, Hindi, Arabic, and Spanish).
8. Host food festivals with different foods provided by diaspora churches and host "fusion" food contests. Invite non-Christian friends to these events.
9. Partner with Christians from different diaspora groups to visit fusion restaurants to share the gospel with the people there.
10. Create a huge fusion restaurant which features dishes from people of different unreached people groups. The restaurant seeks to attract customers from unreached people groups and serve the needs of unreached people through literature and resource information freely available in the restaurant.

VIII.   Cultural Trait: Bilingual and bi-cultural ARC and ABC

Chinese diaspora Christians who are second or third generation can help to share their experiences and serve other diaspora second or third generation groups. Second and third generation diaspora Christians can team together to reach those of their peers and recent diaspora immigrants.

Ministry ideas:

1. Partner with large American churches to minister to the diaspora groups.
2. Serve as facilitator/connector to help large American churches use their ministries and resources to participate in diaspora ministries.
3. Expand the English ministries in the Chinese churches to include non-Chinese members. Intentionally include non-Chinese/non-white in their leadership to make the congregation more multi-cultural.
4. Mobilize the ARCs and ABCs in the church to take the lead in the cross-cultural ministries. Let the Chinese congregation be a financial and prayer supporter to the ARCs and ABCs as they engage in diaspora ministries. Send members from the Chinese congregation to be part of the ministry team so that the Chinese congregation will be involved not only in financial and prayer support but also be active participants.
5. Do research to find out the problems that immigrants face in the community and seek ways to address problems through biblical means.
6. Financially support local diaspora ministries.
7. Go on short-term mission trips to minister to diaspora groups in other parts of the US.
8. Minister to the same ethnic group that a short-term mission team served overseas. For example, if the church does short-term mission trips to Thailand, they can connect to the Thai church locally or reach out to the Thai people in the community after they return.
9. Start new diaspora ministries locally.
10. Host conferences to bring together 2nd and 3rd generation diaspora Christians to encourage and equip them to reach the diaspora community.

Strategies to Mobilize the Chinese Churches to Engage in Diaspora Ministries

Here are some ideas to mobilize the Chinese churches in the SFBA to engage in diaspora ministries:

1. Expand the international student ministries to include non-Chinese students
   a. Offer to provide the same international student services such as airport pickup and furniture giveaways to non-Chinese international students.

b.   Encourage the Chinese students to invite their non-Chinese classmates to special events that are English based.

c.   Open the free English classes to non-Chinese international students.

d.   Invite non-Chinese international students to an authentic Chinese meal or Chinese festivals hosted by the church.

e.   Partner with international student organizations or international student organizations of other ethnic groups to reach out to the international students of different countries.

f.   Assist other diaspora ministries on campus through financial and prayer support.

g.   Train Chinese Christian faculty or Christian volunteers to minister cross-culturally to other diaspora groups.

h.   Show the Chinese Christians on campus how they can minister cross-culturally as well as to their own people.

2.   Present the vision of diaspora ministries to the Chinese congregation

a.   Show how the early Chinese immigrants were ministered to by the American Christian workers in the areas of education, faith, and sex trafficking and how this should motivate the Chinese Christians to serve other diaspora groups in the same way.

b.   Show how Chinese Christians can minister and reach out to their non-Chinese co-workers such as those from India and the Middle East.

c.   Partner with other ethnic churches to serve the diaspora groups in the community. Invite their pastors to share about their ministries.

d.   Partner with large American churches to minister to the diaspora groups.

e.   Serve as facilitator/connector to help large American churches use their resources to participate in diaspora ministries.

f.   Expand the English ministries in the Chinese churches to include non-Chinese members. Intentionally include non-Chinese members in their leadership to make the congregation more multi-cultural.

g.   Mobilize the ARCs and ABCs in the church to take the lead in cross-cultural ministries. Let the Chinese congregation be a financial and prayer supporter to the ARCs and ABCs as they engage in diaspora ministries. Send members from the Chinese congregation to be part of the ministry team so that the Chinese congregation will be involved not only in financial and prayer support but also be active participants.

h. Do research to find out the problems that immigrants face in the community and seek ways to address problems through biblical means.
i. Allow ethnic Christian fellowship groups without building facilities to use the church facility for their meetings.
j. Financially support local diaspora ministries.
k. Go on short-term mission trips to minister to diaspora groups in other parts of the U.S.
l. Minister to the same ethnic group that a short-term mission team served overseas. For example, if the church does short-term mission trips to Thailand, they can connect to the Thai church locally or reach out to the Thai people in the community after returning from the trip.

3. Start new diaspora ministries
   a. Identify the refugee communities in the area and find ways to serve their needs.
   b. Visit local ethnic restaurants and pray for God to provide opportunities to connect with them.
   c. Start free English classes or classes that would appeal to recent immigrants. English classes are usually the first place to go for wives of overseas assignees.
   d. Partner Chinese and other ethnic churches together to build a community center that would serve the needs of the immigrants in the community and include other ethnic groups in the leadership and staff of the community center. The center can offer free simple health services, translation help, counselors to help with immigration questions, family issues and spiritual issues, classes specifically for women who stay at home while their husbands are working, and child-care facilities.
   e. Plant new churches that have a vision for diaspora ministries.
   f. Host conferences to bring the vision of diaspora ministries to the churches in the SFBA.
   g. Start parachurch ministries to specifically minister to the diaspora groups, especially the unreached and unengaged groups.
   h. Start anti-human trafficking ministries that seek to minister to the victims from diaspora groups.
   i. Start business as mission companies to provide employment and financial support to the diaspora groups.
   j. Start a fellowship or network of church pastors/leaders with a heart for diaspora ministries.

k. Start sports ministries that serve the youth of these diaspora groups and invite the youth from other churches to join.
l. Host summer camps for the children and youth of the diaspora groups.
m. Start day care and after school programs that meet the needs of the children of diaspora groups.
n. Start new scholarships to Christian schools for children of diaspora groups.
o. Host field trips to various amusement parks or museums for children of diaspora groups.
p. Volunteer at community events that attract the various diaspora groups.

Integrating the Relational Paradigm and Cross-cultural Mentoring in Local Cross-Cultural Ministry Training for Chinese Diaspora

Here are the keys from relational paradigm and diaspora mission:

1. Most societies in the majority world are highly relational.
2. God works through relationships in mission work.
3. Our relationships to God and to others are important in mission work.
4. Diaspora missions at the micro level involves love, compassion, Christian hospitality.
5. Diaspora missions at the macro level involves partnership and networking.
6. Diaspora missions is "Great commission" plus "Great commandment."
7. The relational paradigm is shown to be successful with immigrant populations.

Here are the keys from cultural differences, dimensions of culture, and Chinese culture:

1. Each culture has its own ideal behaviors, accepted behaviors, and unacceptable behaviors.
2. The dimensions of culture are: context, activity, authority, relationship, and time.
3. Different cultures have their own worldview and cultural values.

4. The relational paradigm is very relevant in Chinese culture, which is seen as basically a concrete relational culture and uses concrete experience as the way of thinking.
5. We see the value of relationships for Chinese people is woven into the culture.
6. The Chinese people have the following traits: 1) confrontation avoidance, 2) emphasis on relationship, 3) high-context culture, and 4) honor and shame.
7. An "incarnational servanthood" approach by placing mature Christian professionals and business people in China has been effective in outreaches.

Here are the keys from mentoring and cross-cultural leadership:

1. Mentoring is a relational experience in which one person empowers another by sharing God-given resources.
2. The God-given resources can include wisdom, experiences, patterns, habits of obedience, principles, and other.
3. The seven mentoring types/functions are: Discipler, Spiritual Guide, Coach, Counselor, Teacher, Sponsor, and Model.
4. The three dynamics vital to a mentoring relationship are: attraction, responsiveness, and accountability.
5. We adapt to different cultures as we serve cross-culturally by honoring and submitting to one another in love.
6. An effective leader in cross-cultural situations is flexible in their style by assessing the cultural expectations of leaders and followers.
7. Leaders use their gift of leadership by taking initiative to focus, harmonize, and enhance the gifts of others for the sake of developing people and cultivating the kingdom of God.[613]

Five Implications of Integrating Relational Paradigm with Cross-cultural Mentoring

The following five implications can be drawn by integrating relational paradigm with cross-cultural mentoring for Chinese diaspora Christians:

1. The cross-cultural mentor should be someone with real cross-cultural ministry experience. This can be a Chinese Christian who has served as a cross-cultural missionary or a Christian who is not Chinese who has served as a cross-cultural missionary. The best mentor would be a Chinese Christian who has intentionally crossed culture to serve people from other cultures. This mentor can share experiences and stories that

---

[613] Plueddemann, 171.

would inspire and give insight to the Chinese diaspora Christians being mentored.

2. The cross-cultural mentoring activities should be relational and group oriented. The activities should involve group activities if possible. When Chinese diaspora Christians serve together in a group, they are less fearful of going to new places and encountering new circumstances. When there are those to talk to in their native Chinese language, they likely would enjoy the experience more.

3. The mentoring activities should avoid, if possible, shame and losing face in the training. The Chinese diaspora Christians should be built up in an environment where they can be encouraged and affirmed as they learn to serve others cross-culturally. They should not be asked to do things that would cause shame or embarrassment to others. There may be times that they are asked to share the gospel in the face of rejection; the way to share the gospel may be through less confrontational methods, such as praying for the person, serving a need, or inviting them to an event – such as a meal.

4. The cross-cultural mentor can also be an experienced "incarnational ministry" Christian. The mentor would be experienced in building relationships with people who are not of the same culture. They may be marketplace missionaries who truly have a heart to reach people cross-culturally and have success and experience in this type of ministry. The best kind of people would be fellow Chinese diaspora Christians who have intentionally reached out to people who are not of the same culture. This type of mentor may help Chinese diaspora Christians do "incarnational ministry" cross-culturally in their workplace and the community where they live.

5. Cross-cultural mentors are needed for the seven types of mentors:
   a. Discipler – A person who can meet one on one with the mentee or in a group setting to disciple and train the mentee in cross-cultural ministry basics.
   b. Spiritual Guide – A person who would look after the mentee spiritually as the mentee seeks to serve cross-culturally.
   c. Coach – A person who can give the vision and train the mentee in specific skills – such as how to share the gospel with a person of another faith, why we should do cross-cultural diaspora ministry, etc.
   d. Counselor – A person who can encourage and counsel the mentee as he/she learns to serve cross-culturally. This person may also be the Discipler.

e.   Teacher – A person who can teach on a particular area in cross-cultural ministry – such as a particular religion, customs, culture, or community.
f.   Sponsor – A person who is connected to a regional or national organization who can help promote the local cross-cultural ministries or help the mentee participate in wider areas of cross-cultural ministries.
g.   Model – Stories of Chinese Christians who have been cross-cultural missionaries would be very inspirational for the mentees, especially if it's someone who is a Chinese diaspora Christian who has served in local cross-cultural ministries.

From these five implications of integrating the relational paradigm with cross-cultural mentoring, there is great potential to mentor Chinese diaspora Christians for cross-cultural ministries. There is also a lot of work to find the right people and resources to do the mentoring that would empower Chinese diaspora Christians to engage in local cross-cultural ministries.

Summary

For the purpose of equipping diaspora Chinese Christians for cross-cultural ministry, this section covered the background for cross-cultural ministries, diaspora missions, cultural differences, Chinese culture from others' perspectives, building relationships cross-culturally, communicating Christ cross-culturally, and practical suggestions to implement cross-cultural ministries in the overseas Chinese church in the SFBA. By having a vision for diaspora missions, we can move the Chinese churches from ethnocentrism to truly embrace a global vision of sharing Christ with all peoples. Local cross-cultural ministry training is an important part of equipping diaspora Christians to engage in diaspora missions beyond the diaspora. May more diaspora Chinese Christians catch the vision and passion to reach their neighbors who are not from their own culture and be trained in cross-cultural ministry.

Strategies for Chinese churches to minister cross-culturally to other diaspora groups were presented. The main overall strategies were 1) expand the international student ministries to include non-Chinese, 2) present the vision of diaspora ministries to the Chinese congregation, 3) and start new diaspora ministries in the community.

There were seven keys drawn from the topics of relational paradigm and diaspora mission. Also, seven keys were drawn from the topics of cultural differences, dimensions of culture, and Chinese culture. Finally, seven keys were drawn from mentoring and cross-cultural leadership. Five implications were drawn from integrating relational paradigm with cross-cultural mentoring.

From the implications, there is a great potential to develop cross-cultural mentoring for Chinese diaspora Christians to engage in local cross-cultural ministries. However, more work needs to be done to identify the right mentors and resources to do the training so that Chinese diaspora Christians can be empowered to do this mission work.

CHAPTER 6
LOCAL CROSS-CULTURAL MINISTRIES OF TWO SELECTED CHINESE DIASPORA CHURCHES IN THE SFBA

Introduction

In his research, co-author Lei encountered several challenges to find suitable Chinese churches in the SFBA to conduct research on their local cross-cultural ministries. First, because Lei is not in full-time ministry, his contacts and relationships with SFBA Chinese pastors were limited. Second, Lei found the American Chinese church pastor may not be interested in talking about local cross-cultural ministries since it is not a major focus of the America Chinese church. The American Chinese churches may see their mission locally is to reach mainly Chinese people, while their mission globally is to reach Chinese people overseas or partner with missions organizations to do cross-cultural ministries in other countries. However, to do cross-cultural ministries locally does not seem to be a major focus of the American Chinese church. This motivated Lei to conduct the study of Chinese churches in the SFBA through archival and internet website research. Lei was able to research what Chinese churches in the SFBA are doing in local cross-cultural ministries through what was mentioned on the church websites. This allowed Lei to research websites of 142 Chinese churches in the SFBA. After the internet website study was completed for Lei's doctoral dissertation, co-author Wan suggested to Lei to conduct two case studies to validate what he found in the internet website research. What Lei found was there are many more local cross-cultural ministries by Chinese churches in the SFBA that were not mentioned in the church websites. The two case studies show potentially much more local cross-cultural ministry by Chinese churches in the SFBA compared to what was mentioned on church websites.

The first church chosen for case study was Ark Baptist Church. This is a 30 year old church with around 160-170 Sunday attendees. The church has many young families and children. Youth and children make up half of the church. This is co-author Lei's local home church. The pastor of Ark Baptist Church, Pastor Joe, graciously agreed to help with the case study. He helped to review Lei's translation of the church history and "1312" vision. He met with Lei in person to confer regarding the purpose and goal of the case study. He wrote answers to questions from Lei. The success of the case study was due to Pastor Joe's passion for the local community. He wants to see the "1312" area codes experience spiritual revival from God. This spiritual revival would include not only the Chinese people but all the people living in the area. We see from the case study that Ark Baptist Church is a model of what a medium size Chinese church can do in local cross-cultural ministries. Ark Baptist Church represents a typical medium sized Chinese church in the SFBA. According to *The 2008 Report: The Bay Area Chinese Churches Research Project Phase II*, 23.5% of the Chinese churches in the SFBA are 100-200 in attendance. The largest percentage is 30.5% with 50-100 in attendance.[614] In *The 2008 Report*, Ark Baptist Church was listed in the 1-50 attendance category.[615] This shows that Ark Baptist Church has more than doubled in attendance since *The 2008 Report*.

Co-author Lei was interested in Forerunner Christian Church as the second church on which to undertake a case study. In Lei's internet website research, he noticed on Forerunner Christian Church's website, there was mention of several local cross-cultural community outreach activities and also partnership with a well-known missions organization to do local outreach. Lei did not know any of the pastors or leaders at Forerunner Christian Church. He asked Pastor Joe if he could help connect him with Forerunner Christian Church. This is common in Chinese culture to connect with others through established relationships (Guanxi). Pastor Joe, a well-respected Chinese pastor in the SFBA, kindly assisted in connecting Forerunner Christian Church with Lei. Forerunner Christian Church gave the contact for the Senior Pastor Grace. Lei called her to explain the purpose of his study and she referred him to Elder Jupin, an elder of the English congregation. Lei contacted Elder Jupin by phone. Elder Jupin was very helpful and gracious in sharing about the story behind their local cross-cultural ministries. The interviews with Elder Jupin were conducted on the phone in two phone conversations. Lei then emailed the transcripts of the interviews to Elder Jupin for her review and editing. The case study interviews with Elder Jupin were edited by both Elder Jupin and Lei. Forerunner Christian Church, with average Sunday attendance of 380-400 in the Fremont home base, represents a large Chinese church in the Bay Area. In *The 2008 Report*,

---

[614] Chuck and Tseng, eds., 7.
[615] Chuck and Tseng, eds., 20.

Forerunner Christian Church was listed in the 300-plus attendees category[616], which constitutes the largest 10% of the Chinese churches in the Bay Area.[617] The case study of Forerunner Christian Church shows the potential of local cross-cultural ministries of a large Chinese church.

Case One: Ark Baptist Church

History of local cross-cultural ministries

Ark Baptist Church was established on May 29, 1988 as a Chinese Baptist Church, and immediately joined the National Association of Southern Baptists. In 1989, the church was renamed Ark Baptist Church. The church is composed of many families.

Historical timeline of the church.

05/29/1988 Chinese Baptist Church of Sunnyvale was founded. The founding pastor was Pastor Barjona. The church borrowed Trinity Baptist Church in Sunnyvale for their meetings.

02/04/2001 The church moved from Trinity Baptist Church to the Adventist Church in Los Altos.

05/08/2001 "Chinese Baptist Church of Sunnyvale" was renamed "Ark Baptist Church."

02/01/2007 Pastor Barjona Liao retired and was appointed as consulting pastor. Pastor Joe Sun became the pastor.

12/09/2007 The church received the 1312 vision and moved from Adventist Church to San Jose.

02/14/2011 Through an auction, the new church building in Milpitas was purchased.

04/03/2011 The first Sunday worship was held in the new church building in Milpitas.

10/10/2011 Church building remodeling began.

01/31/2012 Church building remodeling completed.

04/08/2012 Church building was dedicated.

The "1312" Vision

Ark Baptist Church received the 1312 vision from God, through Psalm 60, to preach the gospel in the 95131 and 95132 zip code areas of North San Jose. In 2005, the church building where they were renting was being sold, forcing a move. Many difficulties were encountered in finding a new place to meet and they did not know where to go. At this time, God gave them the 1312 vision

---

[616] Chuck and Tseng, eds., 22.
[617] Chuck and Tseng, eds., 7.

through the 60th chapter of Psalms, which not only clearly described their situation at the time but also let them see 95131 and 95132 zip code areas as the place where God was leading them. The two zip codes in North San Jose Valley are separated by Highway 680 and was their "Edom." Living in this small four-square mile area were 12,000 Chinese people, as in Psalm 60 when Joab described the 12,000 Edomites. There was only one small Chinese church in the area at the time; it was decided to move to the "1312" area to preach the gospel.

The church found the 1312 zip code not an easy place to settle. Due to the restrictions of San Jose city government planning zoning, it was a difficult area to find a suitable location to establish the church. God let them see an industrial building in 1312 that was one of the few buildings that could be converted into a church. After they prayed, the decision was made to rent and remodel. The process was very bumpy. Lease talk took more than half a year; the application for the license of the church took more than a year, costing more than $100,000. During the period, an unprecedented strike by municipal government inspectors was encountered. God finally brought them to the "1312" area. On the second day after receiving the license, the church devotion schedule fell on Psalm 60 and they were amazed by God's timely reminder.

Since relocating to the "1312" building at the end of 2007, the church prayed for the revival of the "1312" area. They actively entered the community and organize a number of events to attract people to know God. Also, the pastor of the church visited the pastors of American churches in the area and prayed with them for the revival of 1312 area. However, just one year later, on January 1, 2009, they suddenly received a letter from Tzu Chi Foundation telling them that they had bought the entire building and became their landlord. The brothers and sisters were all stunned and, as in Psalm 60:1, their question was "God, have you rejected us?" There were many houses in the Bay Area, they wondered "Why did this happen to us?" They had only been there for a year. Though encountering many miraculous signs in their church relocating process, there were many doubts and fears after acquiring the new landlord. God reaffirmed His promise to them through Isaiah 41:9-10 "I took you from the ends of the earth, from its farthest corners I called you. I said, 'You are my servant'; I have chosen you and have not rejected you. So, do not fear, for I am with you; do not be dismayed, for I am your God. I will strengthen you and help you; I will uphold you with My righteous right hand" (NIV). These promises from God enabled them to stand firm through these most difficult times.

After prayer and discussions, the church gradually attained the consensus to buy a building to fulfill the "1312" vision God had entrusted to them. Following a year and half of searching, they suddenly found an industrial building at the junction of San Jose and Milpitas. This is positioned in the 1312 area and is closer to the populace of the residential area than the original location. The internal structure was in full compliance of the conditions they had listed. It could be said to be 100% tailor-made for them. The lot had been planned as a high-density commercial residential area. The prospects were promising; however, the price was 2.8 million. The church only had $80,000 in their building fund. After investigating the site and praying, the decision was reached to purchase by faith and bid with three other buyers. At this time, God gave them two passages to confirm that this was the "Promise land" He was giving to them. At the moment before the bid, they received the words from Psalm 24:1, "The earth is the Lord's, and everything in it, the world, and all who live in it." On the eve of the seller's selection of the buyer, they received the words from Isaiah 45:3, "I will give you hidden treasures, riches stored in secret places, so that you may know that I am the Lord, the God of Israel, who summons you by name."

Collectively, they held their breath and waited for the results, then were told they had been chosen out of the four buyers. They were overjoyed. They immediately signed a contract and actively started the task of fundraising.

Nevertheless, the signing of the contract was not smooth. Due to the unclear property rights of the building and the seller's reluctance to clarify the property rights, it was impossible to reach an agreement after repeated negotiations. Finally, the seller categorically left the talks and negotiated with other buyers. This was undoubtedly discouraging for all. However, it was heard that the seller owed the bank a loan and the building faced being auctioned by the bank. Therefore, the church body changed directions and waited for the auction. The hope was to buy the property with clear property rights through auction and prayers were raised in the hope that this building would not be bought by others. Unexpectedly, immediately before the bank held the auction, the seller opened a company, transferred the property rights to the new company and declared bankruptcy, freezing the assets so that the bank could not auction it. The owner was caught in a bankruptcy lawsuit. The bank scheduled an auction four times with each blocked by bankruptcy lawsuits. The church could not see their way forward, and only relied on God's promise that "I will help you," continuing to wait. The brothers and sisters gathered at noon every day to pray.

Six months later, on January 31, 2011, the judge finally sentenced, the bank won the case, and the auction ensued. They were very excited for this opportunity for which they had been preparing. However, when they rushed to the court for the fifth auction, they heard the auction was cancelled because the seller once again declared bankruptcy in the same way. This news caused them to fall into deeper disappointment. For how many more bankruptcies should they wait? What if someone else purchased this building in the process? They thanked God that the judge revoked the case on the third day. The bank was scheduled to have the sixth auction on Valentine's Day February 14, 2011.

On the day of the auction, they were ready to go to court. When the building was read, it was not cancelled. The process took less than half a minute. They bid a penny above the starting price, which is less than half of the seller's original offer price. They were ecstatic like those who had dreamed. After eight months of difficulties and waiting, they finally received their hidden treasure from God. They gave glory to God for His wisdom and faithfulness.

After obtaining the building, they immediately started to rebuild and applied for the reconstruction license. Due to the diligent attitude and rich experiences of the contractor, the reconstruction project progressed rapidly and was completed in three and a half months. On February 19, 2012, one year after the auction of the building, they were able to hold their Sunday worship in the lobby for the first time. On April 08, 2012, Easter Sunday, they had a thanksgiving ceremony and dedicated this church to God.

In the past years, God has repeatedly placed Ark Baptist Church in extremely difficult situations, leaving them no choice but to rely closely on God, to believe in His promises, and to see His power. The new church building once again confirmed the call of the 1312 vision. They believe God will lead them to win people to Christ in this region and that revival will surely come to 1312 as they keep crying out to God.

(Translated from Chinese based on information from the Church website: http://www.arkbaptistchurch.org)

Operation of local cross-cultural ministries

Ark Baptist Church begin to have English translation services in 2001 to serve non-Chinese speaking members and attendees. The church started participating in community service in 2014.

Recently, the church hosted a local Bible Bee study for children and youth, and Scriptorium for adults and families, inviting local Christians to come participate. Those who came to participate included Asian Indian, Caucasian, and Japanese. The church had mixed couples, with spouses who are Caucasian or Indian coming to services and listening to the English translation. During Christmas time, members walked to local residential communities to invite them to the Christmas program by hanging door hangers with a blessing message. The church participated in Milpitas Care and helped to clean up area parks. In addition, they invited local high school students to join the clean-up efforts to fulfill the students' community service requirements. The church participated in planning of the National Day of Prayer rally with other local American and ethnic churches. Members of the church volunteered to tutor students at a local elementary school. Twice a year, the church hosts evangelistic activities in front of a local Chinese supermarket in the Milpitas Square shopping center. They handed out tracts and balloons and reached out to not only the Chinese shoppers but others as well, including Hispanic, Asians, and Caucasian shoppers. The church also raised money for CityTeam ministries once each year to give backpacks to the needy.

118

The pastor of the church, Pastor Joe Sun, regularly meets with 10 local pastors in Milpitas for retreat and to plan the National Day of Prayer activities. Area pastors include Vietnamese, Korean, India, Chinese, Filipino, and Caucasian.

Pastor Sun also mentioned other local cross-cultural ministries of the church which included non-Chinese such as the College student group, Easter Park Egg Hunt, Shine Character Camp, Fasting & Prayer Camp, and Thanksgiving Hot Pot. The College student group included friends of college students who are not Chinese. The Easter Park Egg Hunt in a local park drew children from the neighborhood and those walking by the park. The Shine Character Camp also had non-Chinese children join. The Fasting & Prayer Camp was held with an American church. The Thanksgiving Hot Pot included non-Chinese friends of church members.

The church also offered a meeting place for the neighborhood Homeowner Association (HOA) and Affordable Housing Community meetings. These meetings would be attended by people from the diverse local community.

Challenges of Chinese Church local cross-cultural ministries

What do you see are the challenges of local cross-cultural ministries?

Pastor Joe Sun:

Most Chinese churches consist of first generation immigrants; they came to the United States to pursue better quality life and to fulfill their American dreams. Their focus is to settle in this foreign land and thrive with good fortune and better lives. Usually they don't care too much about the society and they don't get involved. Most church members only care about the "success" of their own church; they want to reap what they sowed; they don't even connect with other Chinese churches, let alone churches of different ethnicities. Connecting with the local community will be put as the last priority because they see themselves as strangers in this land. Basically, Chinese churches in America seldom get involved with the community and often isolate themselves from the whole society, including other churches of different ethnicities.

With that being said, the biggest challenge to promote cross-cultural ministries in Chinese churches is to change the perspective of the leaders and members. It's hard for them to grasp the idea that they are the priests of this land and are ordained as the focal point between the heaven and the earth. They are responsible for spreading the Gospel to everyone who lives around them regardless of their nationalities. How to change the perspective of the church leaders and its members is the first challenge that needs to be addressed.

Secondly, it's challenging to actually implement cross-cultural ministries in Chinese churches. Due to language barriers, churches typically put the cross-cultural ministries on the plate of the English group. However, the leaders of the Chinese congregation tend to control all the ministries. The English congregations in Chinese churches often complain about the restrictions that are put on them. Sometimes they feel that they are less respected. That's why the English pastors in Chinese churches usually don't stay long. It's hard to retain the English pastors, and it's even harder to develop cross-cultural ministries in Chinese churches.

Vision of Chinese Church local cross-cultural ministries

What do you see the church do in local cross-cultural ministries in the near and distant future?

Pastor Joe Sun:

One of our church's main visions is to connect the older and the younger generations. We usually promote ministries through family settings where parents and children work together in things like community services, leading worship, prayers, and even after meal cleanup. To bring two generations together we have to establish a bi-lingual environment in the church. This is something we can leverage to build cross-cultural ministries. In the past, we have hosted many children and youth events in English which attracted people of different cultural backgrounds from the neighborhood. We also have members with non-Chinese spouses in our church. We need to create a bi-lingual environment for them.

In the near future we would like to keep developing a bi-lingual environment to attract different cultural groups. It would be ideal to have our Sunday messages delivered in both English and Chinese, 50% of the time in each language with translation. Eventually we hope to build a church where English speaking people of different cultures will feel welcome and belong and are comfortable enough to stay. We have an English college student group now, and we hope someday we can have English adult small groups and English prayer meetings in addition to the bi-lingual worship services.

North San Jose area is a unique place in California, it's even more unique in the whole United States; many immigrants have moved in from different parts of the world, and Caucasians are becoming a minority in this region. We truly hope that we can attract people of different cultures. By presenting our family core values with the many English-speaking children, and through the endeavor of building a bi-lingual environment, people of different cultures might be comfortable to interact with us, and the Gospel could be spread as a result.

Contextualization of diaspora mission and cross-cultural training

The goal of relational paradigm is to have healthy and appropriate relationships with each other and with the Triune God.[618] Relational missionary training measures the outcome by the relationships between the various parties involved.[619] Wan and Hedinger list seven key missionary relationships: 1) Relationships within the Trinity, 2) Relationships between the Trinity and the missionary that He sends to the nations, 3) Relationships between the Trinity and the audience, 4) Relationships between the missionary and the audience, 5) Relationships between the missionary and his/her home culture, 6) Relationships between the audience and his/her culture, and 7) An appropriate relationship with evil spirits.[620]

From Ark Baptist Church, we see the #1 relationships within the Trinity by the work of salvation in the founding members and the establishment of the church through Pastor Barjona Liao in 1988. We see the #2 relationships between the Trinity and the missionary that He sends to the nations by the journey of the church from Sunnyvale to Milpitas. The church changed its name from "Chinese Baptist Church of Sunnyvale" to "Ark Baptist Church" in 2001, which prepared the church to serve all people in the place where they would settle. The "1312 vision" to preach the gospel in the 95131 and 95132 zip code areas of North San Jose was received from God in 2005 when the church was compelled to move. God gave them the 1312 vision through a chapter in Psalms from the Bible, which prompts them to see God's plan for their situation at the time as well as the 95131 and 95132 zip code areas as the place God wants them to preach the gospel. We see the #3 relationships between the Trinity and the audience by lows and highs of the journey of the church to find a place to settle in order to fulfill the 1312 vision. We see the #4 relationships between the missionary and the audience in the leadership of the pastors of the church seeking the Lord and trusting in the Lord through their challenges and disappointments. We see the #5 relationships between the missionary and his/her home culture in Chinese ministries of the first generation. We see the

---

[618] Wan and Hedinger, 291.
[619] Wan and Hedinger, 291.
[620] Wan and Hedinger, 284-285.

#6 relationships between the audience and his/her culture in the bilingual efforts of the church. The pastor is connecting to local pastors from different ethnic backgrounds and leading the church toward a bilingual environment in order to fulfill God's calling for them. We see #7, an appropriate relationship with evil spirits, by the fervent prayers of the church as they faced challenges moving from Sunnyvale to Milpitas.

Case Two: Forerunner Christian Church

History of local cross-cultural ministries

Jupin, an Elder of the English ministry at Forerunner Christian Church (Forerunner) tells the story of how the church got started in local cross-cultural ministries and how breakthroughs between the Chinese ministry and English ministry members helped them on their journey to become an "International Family."

Forerunner Christian Church moved from Milpitas to Fremont in June of 2004. Pastor Grace felt the burden to change our name from Zion Church of Praise to Forerunner Christian Church. This echoes the Jewish tradition that people often receive a new name to reflect change or enlargement of their calling and destiny. We changed our name, and along with that we also changed a lot of other things such as our vision. Our vision became a lot more global. Pastor Grace, who planted this church, was a missionary from Taiwan. It was such a miracle how we moved to Fremont.

After moving to Fremont, we joined CityServe Pastors' Network. This is a network of pastors in the Tri-city area – Fremont, Newark, and Union City. I believe this has been going for around 30 years. The pastors get together monthly to have lunch. They have a weekly pastors' prayer meeting. It is interdenominational – Methodist, Presbyterian, Charismatic, Baptist, Pentecostal, etc. We are all gathered together as pastors. Part of the Pastors' Network is to serve the needs of the city. So, one offshoot of Pastors' Network is Compassion Network. Compassion Network is a local non-profit organization that actually came out of the pastors' church planting in the city. The pastors were asking, "How we can serve our city?" Compassion Network is like a hub or center where the needs of the city filter through. There's an office that receives the needs of families and individuals, interviews them, screens them, makes sure it's official, works with the city of Fremont, and then sends out every week an email blast to all the local churches saying something like "We have a mom who needs gas, so she can go to work, sitting in her car right now." All the churches in Compassion

Network are part of this network of 40-plus ministries. We have a coordinator at every church who will respond, such as "we have a family who wants to meet that need." Compassion Network will connect that one family with the needy family and they can do the ministry. Compassion Network is a gathering place for the needs of the city and for the people of the church to meet them. Forerunner is part of this network. When we moved to Fremont, we joined Compassion Network and CityServe. This is one way we are connected to meet the local needs of the city.

Language is an issue because all the senior level pastors were first generation immigrant Christians. They have a heart to serve, but they ask, "How do we do that?" We did it at the beginning through giving. For example, for Thanksgiving we sponsored 100 Thanksgiving turkey meals for $75-$80. We collect the money and give it to Compassion Network to buy the meals. Another church distributes the meals and shares the gospel to the families coming to receive the meals. So, in the beginning a lot of our involvement was financial. We've given a lot in this way.

Somewhere along the way, Pastor Grace wanted to lift up the English Ministry in the midst of Forerunner. One of the mandates of the English Ministry, being fluent in English, is to engage with the community on behalf of Forerunner. We heard a call from CityServe – "What if every church in the city adopts a school around the neighborhood. The church would make her presence known. "We are praying for you. Is there something we can help you with?" CityServe sees that if every church would do that then the whole city will be covered. When Pastor Grace and other leaders of the church heard this call, we felt like we wanted to do that. So, we adopted our local elementary school. For the first three years, we were very active. The whole church resourced the English ministry to engage with the school principal. The school had a new principal who is a believer. The principal couldn't believe we would help the school and she had been praying to God. She said, "We need backpacks." We asked the church and they would bring backpacks and school supplies and donate money. We asked this Caucasian principal to come to our church on Sunday because we wanted to pray for her. So, she came. And she was in the Mandarin service. She was one of the few Caucasian who were there. Our whole church raised our hands to bless her, acknowledge her calling, and bless her school. She was crying. She couldn't believe it. We continued the relationship with the school. We sent teams of volunteers to help them with their afterschool program. We brought our teenagers in to help the students who were from low socio-economic homes. This was part of the tutoring program. We also helped provide snacks during their testing time. During Teacher's appreciation Day, we would host a lunch for the teachers. During Christmas time, we would go there with presents.

We would post banners to welcome the students back to school. That's how we engaged with the school we adopted.

Our pastors were convicted that what if God were to take our church away from this neighborhood, would people notice? If the neighbors don't even notice if we are gone, what is the purpose of us being located right here? We wanted to have an impact. We wanted to be *so* a part of the neighborhood that if we were not here, they would be like, "Oh no! They can't go because they have been such a light to the neighborhood." That was our heart. The adoption of the elementary school was just one example of how we serve our neighbors. We have gang activities in the neighborhood around our church. We felt like if we reach the elementary students while their hearts are open, then they would recognize who we are – "That was the church that tutored and helped us. That's someone we know." So, it would be like a friendship. This friendship may reduce the gang activities in the area.

We engaged with this elementary school ministry for four years and the fifth year we didn't do as much because the person doing the coordination got a full-time job. We are still here. So, the principal would email us to ask us to help with events like a Back-to-School night. The principal knows we are here and she can reach out to us.

The English ministry is 50-70 people. Half of the members are youth. It is only in the past 3-4 years we have stable married family couples. We have 10 stable couples and families, either English only or bi-racial couple. A few years ago, we had a Kyrgyzstan family. We had a Korean family. We have an Indian Christian family. We have members who are Vietnamese, Caucasian, Hispanic, Filipino, and Middle Eastern. Not every family is bi-racial. The Indian family just saw our church, and came, and it felt like home.

The story behind this is not how a Chinese church engages with the neighborhood. For a long time our pastor wanted to engage with the neighborhood by investing in the second-generation to go into the neighborhood. We hosted YWAM and our whole church, whether you spoke English or not, went. We have 120-plus people going to the neighborhood to knock on doors, offering to pray, and sharing the gospel to anyone who is open. It is not easy for a Chinese church to do that.

Our pastors and leaders always wanted to raise up a second-generation. Our senior leaders really wanted to pass on the core values or inheritance God has given to us to the second-generation. I'm part of the second-generation team. At the core leadership meeting a few years ago, Pastor Grace invited all the second-generation leaders. We began to pray together. We did that for a year. It was challenging because people in the second-generation did not speak Chinese well or at all. During leadership meetings, we always needed to have translators. Literally people would be translating at the same time, even while praying. In the beginning, we felt there was a distance between us and our senior leaders. We respected our senior leaders yet there wasn't like a heart connect. We were together, like we were coworkers, but we were not really family. We were in the family of God, we were ministry leaders, but we were not close. It took us about a year to press through in this uncomfortable setting. When you choose a song, are you going to choose a Chinese song or an English song? Even things as simple as that. Do you translate all the prayers? How about when English speakers pray? We've gone through that process so that we can be together.

At one of the meetings, when we were praying, our senior pastoral leaders started to connect with the Homecoming Movement with Pastor David Demian. The Homecoming Movement is all about how we can live as a family again. Churches are many times like orphanages, because we come to know the Lord then we realize we are broken. So we are a whole bunch of broken people who know what grace looks like. Here we are, trying to love each other. We are still in the process of healing. But we don't know how to be family. Pastor Grace felt convicted and wanted to bring the second-generation in, "Even though it's messy; we want you guys in." Somewhere along that process our senior leaders actually repented to us, during one of the core leaders' meetings. They repented of not knowing how to love us well. They would give us resources whenever we needed, but they didn't know how to connect their heart with us, how to communicate with us. They recognized because of cultural differences, even their heart intended well, nevertheless they have hurt us as the second-generation. When they repented to us (the second-generation leaders), something broke. Like Malachi 4, the hearts of the fathers turn to the children and the children turn to their fathers. I felt like that was the beginning of something. One of the second-generation leaders started crying out loud. What came out of that person's mouth was, "You say you love, but you never intended to stay here in America. You are always thinking of America as a place for ministry. Once you are done, you are going to go back to China. You are going to go back to Taiwan. We are just going to be orphans right here. You don't see this land as your home. But we are born here. We are raised here. We think this is home. But for you this is just a place for ministry. When you are old, you are just going to retire back to Taiwan or China." When that leader said that, it was like God was doing something. Then the other second-generation leaders started crying. It was like God was doing some healing. We had probably about 30 leaders – pastors, ministers, elders. Our senior leaders started crying too. We started repenting. We repented to God that we never owned America as our home. We always saw it as a place where we minister then we will leave. At that time, we felt it was important to pray for America, for the election, for the president. And God was convicting our senior leaders that they have no authority to pray for America because they don't own her. The leaders see this as a land where they are not going to stay. The understanding was, "You don't own America. If you don't own America, how can you have authority to pray for her?" That was such a big breakthrough for us as a church leadership team.

From that day forward, there was a shift. Our senior pastors, even though their English is not that good, would try to speak to us during Sunday service – to the English ministry. They would try to connect hearts over tasks, as senior leaders to come into the English ministry to oversee the English ministry, instead of having the second-generation wholly on their own. They really believed that the second-generation leaders were so capable: just give them resources, they can do it on their own. We say we want spiritual mothers and fathers. We need the covering of the first-generation as we carry God's legacy and the calling together.

At one of our Core meetings, our youth minister also confessed feeling like she is being used because of her English skills. She felt she was being treated as a coworker, like a ministry leader, a hired hand. She repented of that and says, "I want to be your daughter. I want to own you as my spiritual parents. I want to see this as my home and my family. I want to have your inheritance and carry on your legacy in the Lord. I want to have what you have." When she had that heart turn, the whole youth ministry was turned around. Before it was, "why do we do it like that, that's the old way, I want to do it this way. This is more relevant to the kids." After she had that heart turning, there was alignment. She began to teach and share the inner life teachings from her heart.

Several years ago, God prophesied over our church – You are going to be an International Family, Forerunner will be an International Family Center. Israeli pastors ministering in the Middle East. will go through this house and be refreshed and be sent out again. We wondered how that would happen? We are barely starting to learn how to love each other. We felt God saying, "Yes, that is what I want. Before it wasn't a family, it was a ministry. But now I'm working in your hearts so that you will be family."

This was such a big shift in our core leaders – for the first-generation and second-generation. We have meals together, not because we have ministry meetings. I would go shopping and call up my elder and ask what I can buy for her. Or call up the worship pastor and ask should I pick up this or that for you? We do that for each other now. That is a big huge change for us.

For our church, as you asked, how does a Chinese church minister in an English environment? Right now, God opened a door. Every quarter, Pastor

Grace gathers with a core contingent of pastors. There are Hispanics, Israelis, those formerly from other religions, Caucasians, Native Americans, about 30 pastors. This is independent from the English ministry. These international pastors are Pastor Grace's friends. All of this happened in the past five years – us learning to be family. Even as we engage with the multi-cultures around us, it's because there's been a heart change. Our senior leaders own America as their home now. Since they own America as their home, the second generation says they feel secure. "We understand that you are not going to plant a church and leave us." You will understand when I send you the ministries we do. I feel like God is more interested in the heart of His children when we respond as the first and second generation. What does that look like? I feel like God has done a lot. The result of our ministry is a consequence of the heart change in the core leadership level. That is the core of what we do right now. Why the second generation goes out to the community now.

Operation of local cross-cultural ministries

1. What are other ministries or activities that serve/include non-Chinese people? i.e. community service, outreaches, programs, sports, social events, neighborhood events, etc.?

Elder Jupin:

Here is a list of what I know (and is not comprehensive) of the outreach activities FRCC does. Somewhere in there should also be "Love SF," where we send young adults to SF to join YWAM to reach the city with street evangelism. I think we did it twice.

FRCC COMMUNITY OUTREACH

Neighborhood/City Outreach
Spring Carnival (April)
*game booths, carnival snacks, bounce houses, prophetic readings, etc. for the neighborhood
Harvest Festival/Halloween (October)
*game booths, carnival snacks, bounce houses, prophetic readings, etc. for the neighborhood
Reverse Trick-O-Treat/Halloween (October)
*go through the neighborhood to give out LED lights/candies and do prophetic treasure hunting/prayers of blessing
Mail letters to the neighbors around FRCC to notify of special events/English-speaking conferences
Visit surrounding neighbors door to door with small gifts

Host StarKids after school program, academic enrichment (Mostly Indian families)

IFY non-profit after school enrichment program/Chinese school (Mostly Chinese families) on campus, year-round

School Outreach @ Brier Elementary

2013/14 Year-long Monday Tutoring Program (Bronco Brainiacs)
*30 students, two hours, some FRCC youth, some local high school students (Community Service hours for the High school students/outreach)
2012/13 Year-long Board Game Room (Bronco Brainiacs)
*90 students, teach characters and cooperation through structured board-games
Special event support
Student store, Book Faire, "Mad Science" yard sale

Donations/Fundraising

*Technology, backpacks, school supplies (raised $10,000 in house)
*Collected donations FRCC church-wide to help with yard sale to fund raise for science enrichment

For Staff - encouragement cards, dessert days, luncheons, gifts for teacher appreciation

Compassion Network

Collection Drives
*2013 Shoe Pantry
FRCC church-wide collection for shoes for the needy
*2012 Cereal Drive
(youth group)
Collecting dry-goods for the needy
*Bountiful Harvest (Nov)
Yearly sponsoring 100 Turkey dinners for needy families at Thanksgiving, and delivering the meals (at Cedars Church)
*Tree of Hope (Dec)
Collecting Christmas gifts for the needy families, and distributing the gifts (at Bridges Church)
Weekly E-Blasts
Individual FRCC members can respond to postings on FRCC website for needs screened by Compassion Network (either services or item donations)
Winter Homeless shelter (winter) + Soup Kitchen (Community center)
*Donating three weeks of daily dinners for eight homeless/security guard
*Outreach to the men by eating dinner, leading worship service at the shelter
CityServe Pastors
Disaster Preparedness Conference (MPR)

*Hosting community training on site from Fremont Fire Department EMT, local disaster preparedness agencies to help church staff to be ready in times of disaster

Monthly CityServe Pastors' Luncheon
*Hosting Monthly luncheons (on site) for Tri-city area pastors/ministries to gather and connect
*Weekly city pastors' prayer

YWAM Missionaries (2013?)
*Provide housing
*Support logistically
* door-to-door evangelism

Welcome new churches in the neighborhood with desserts/flowers, cakes

Fire Station Outreach (Nov)
*Delivering pumpkin pies to all the Fire Stations in Fremont, and send teams to thank and bless the Fremont Fire Department

Retirement Community/Hospital Outreach
*usually during Christmas, children's ministry

Churches would have a liaison to receive the weekly E-blast and forward to the members who are interested in reaching out to the city outside of the church walls.

Here is an example below:

--

Dear family,

Hope you are having a great week! Thank you for taking the time to read this blast. Please let me know if you are interested in volunteering or giving to one of the requests below. See attached file for more information. Thank you!

May God give you the desires of your heart!
Judy

URGENT NEED: Driver/Companion for a day. Client had seizure and needs someone to spend a day with her in Hayward county court.

GROUP NEED: Client has heart issues. Need a group to help clean and organize shed.

DONATION REQUEST:

Gas to get to appointments	Mom-to-be is homeless and living in car. Needs gas to get to doctor appointments. She's a high-risk patient. Once she's delivered, Abode will try to find her a place.

2. What do you see are the challenges of local cross-cultural ministries?

Elder Jupin:

Speaking for my church, I see the key is how much we own that revelation of the sea of glass. The Lamb of God is there and one day every tongue, tribe, people, color who are redeemed will worship on that sea of glass for eternity. How is my heart, my church as a church family relating to that passage? As immigrants (I'm also a first generation; I came when I was eleven), it's really about how much our hearts and minds engaged with that revelation. As an immigrant church, we may feel we are "just" an immigrant, so we want to stay in the immigrant church and nourish one another, and then we can be successful out there. We never see "out there" as part of our inheritance. "Out there" is seen as a challenge and we conquer it. It is rarely part of "my inheritance" or "my family." When we broke that boundary through the Homecoming Movement, we began to own the revelation that God has sent us, as Chinese immigrants, here to America, for His Kingdom purpose. In His excellent wisdom, He chose us as a Chinese people in the Bay Area to accomplish that plan in THIS land. We were challenged to own our place in this land, to take responsibility for it, to invest in it, and to "feel" with our hearts when bad things happen to this land. We began to pray earnestly each week for the elections, the California assembly bills, and specific events happening in our State and Nation.

Pray the Malachi 4 passage. For many years, we did not understand what it meant - turning the hearts of the fathers to the children and the hearts of the children to the fathers.

The whole Homecoming Movement made such a huge impact on our church as we began to repent. To see that God is not only satisfied with the Chinese, that He put us here for a purpose – in this white and Indian neighborhood for a purpose. So, we want to be a part of that. There is a family out there that is not my color, what am I to do with that? For my pastor, it starts from the top down. When my pastor began to take hold of that passage, God opened the doors for her to connect globally with non-Chinese pastors, even with her broken English. She has really good pastor friends now who are white and Egyptian and Arabs and Jews, and they meet regularly not because they are in the same denomination or ministry projects; they meet to connect relationally. That is so unusual for a Chinese immigrant pastor over a Chinese church, don't you think?

3. What do you see the church do in local cross-cultural ministries in the near and distant future?

Elder Jupin:

We definitely have a very Indian community. In the community, the Indians and Chinese are very alike, such as striving for excellence. This September, one of our sisters' non-profit organizations, IFY, moved into our church. This sister was a top-level minister at our church, but God called her to start this non-profit after school program. She rented another property for three years. This year her non-profit organization moved to the church campus. We renovated an entire wing of the church for the afterschool program. You can tell, it is all painted blue. We realized our outreach starts with the afterschool Chinese school for the Chinese community. We have classes for art, chess, programming, etc.

For different classes, we are beginning to see different communities wanting to come in and be part of it. The most recent one is the Hip-Hop class. The pastor's son Jensen is a professional dancer who competes in Hip-Hop competitions. He started teaching here and the students he taught in another school followed him here. These Indian students and families are coming to the church. They like Jensen so they are coming on a weeknight to take two hours of Hip-Hop dancing class. We didn't realize that all of a sudden it was going to draw a crowd. Now they are here, what are we going to do? So, we see this as an opportunity because we don't get to talk with Indian parents outside of work or school. Some people would come a little early to make friends with them.

There is a local pastor who has a heart for a local ethnic community. He is teaching a weekend guitar class. His students currently are all Indians. We just open the doors. I find that as we open the door, we open our hearts. There isn't really a need for a program. We just open our door and see this is what God is doing. And this is what we do as God's children.

Right now, we don't have a very solid English children's program. So, I could see that in the future we will need to have a very solid English children's program as follow-up. We have English ministries for the youth and onward. We are really solid in that. We don't have a children's program that is in English exclusively because most of our children, except for a few, are bilingual. Most of the children are semi-able to understand Chinese. So, I think we really need to respond to that need. There are three of my neighbors who are Indians, who ask me about the classes we have. I told her this is what we teach the kids and that Jesus is the only God. She was really interested to learn. We thought that the guitar class would be good if she wants to come for free music class. We have program for her friend's youth, but no program for the younger ones yet.

Contextualization of diaspora mission and cross-cultural training

Based on the seven key missionary relationships (Wan and Hedinger), the following can be seen from the Forerunner Christian Church case study. We see the #1 relationships within the Trinity by the work of salvation in the founding members and the establishment of the church through Pastor Grace. We see the #2 relationships between the Trinity and the missionary that He sends to the nations in the move from Milpitas to Fremont in 2004 and the giving of a new name and a global vision. We see the #3 relationships between the Trinity and the audience by the work of the Holy Spirit in the Homecoming Movement to convict the first-generation senior leaders and second-generation English ministry leaders of the gaps in their relationships. Only when the relationships are restored and strengthened within the church can they have the passion to reach out to the neighborhoods. We see the #4 relationships between the missionary and the audience in the Homecoming Movement and how it impacted the leaders and spread to the whole church to give them a passion to serve the various ethnic people in the community. We see the #5 relationships between the missionary and his/her home culture in the Chinese ministry at Forerunner Christian Church and the role of the Senior pastor to cast a global multi-cultural vision to the Chinese congregation. We see the #6 relationships between the audience and his/her culture in the Forerunner Christian Church English ministry and the multi-cultural outreaches and ministries in the diverse ethnic community. We see #7, an appropriate relationship with evil spirits by challenges they face in the neighborhood such as the gang problem. They are going to the schools to serve and establishing relationships with the elementary students as light and salt in the community.

Missiological Implications from the Two Cases

The two case studies have the following 10 common themes:
1) Church was started by Chinese pastor from overseas
2) Church moved to a new location with a new vision
3) Pastor joined local pastors' network

4) Desire for a bilingual environment to connect the first and second generation

5) Cross-cultural ministry in community service

6) Cross-cultural ministry in evangelism

7) Cross-cultural ministry in church activities

8) Passion to reach the local people in the community for Christ

9) An emphasis on the family

10) Needs in cross-cultural ministry.

Common Themes	Ark Baptist Church	Forerunner Christian Church
1. Church started by Chinese pastor from overseas	Pastor Barjona was a pastor from Taiwan	Pastor Grace was a missionary from Taiwan
2. Church moved to new location with new name, vision	Church moved from Sunnyvale to Los Altos, then to San Jose/Milpitas after receiving the "1312 vision" to preach the gospel in the 95131 and 95132 zip code areas of North San Jose. Church name changed from "Chinese Baptist Church of Sunnyvale" to "Ark Baptist Church."	Church moved from Milpitas to Fremont. Church name was changed from "Zion Church of Praise" to "Forerunner Christian Church." Their vision became a lot more global.
3. Pastor joined local pastors' network	Pastor Joe joined 10 local pastors in Milpitas for retreat and to plan the National Day of Prayer activities. Pastors include Vietnamese, Korean, Asian Indian, Chinese, Pilipino, and Caucasian.	After moving to Fremont, the pastors joined CityServe Pastors Network – an interdenominational network in the Tri-city area – Fremont, Newark, and Union City. The pastors get together for lunch monthly and have weekly pastors' prayer meeting.

Common Themes	Ark Baptist Church	Forerunner Christian Church
4. Implement a bilingual environment to connect first and second generation	Implement bilingual Chinese/English environment to bring the first and second generations together, such as bilingual Sunday messages.	Implement bilingual Chinese/English environment in the core leaders' meeting to bring in the second-generation leaders.
5. Cross-cultural ministry in community service	-Milpitas Care -Tutoring in elementary school -Raise money for City team ministries -Meeting place for neighborhood Home Owner Association (HOA) and Affordable Housing Community meetings. -Easter Park Egg Hunt	-Tutoring @ Brier Elementary -Special events @Brier Elementary -Donations/fundraising @Brier Elementary; -Ministry to Staff @Brier Elementary; -Shoe Pantry; -Cereal Drive -Bountiful Harvest; -Tree of Hope -Weekly E-Blasts; -Winter Homeless shelter + Soup Kitchen; -Disaster Preparedness Conference; -Monthly CityServe Pastors' Luncheon; -Welcome new churches; -Fire Station Outreach -Retirement Community/Hospital Outreach
6. Cross-cultural ministry in evangelism	-Local Chinese supermarket evangelism -Christmas program neighborhood invitation -National Day of Prayer rally	-Reverse Trick-O-Treat/Halloween -Mail letters -Visited surrounding neighbors -YWAM Missionaries
7. Cross-cultural ministry in church activities	-Bilingual Sunday message -Local Bible Bee -Local Scriptorium	-English congregation -Spring Carnival -Harvest Festival/Halloween -Hosting StarKids

Common Themes	Ark Baptist Church	Forerunner Christian Church
	-College student group -Shine Character Camp -Fasting & Prayer Camp -Thanksgiving Hotpot	-IFY
8. Passion to reach the local people in the community for Christ	-"1312 vision" for evangelism and revival in the 95131 and 95132 zip code areas of North San Jose -Pastor Joe joined local pastors for retreat and to plan the National Day of Prayer activities.	-Joined CityServe Pastors' Network to serve the city. -Be a light in the community through adopting a local elementary school. -Second generation going out to the community to serve.
9. An emphasis on the family	-One of the church's main visions is to connect the older and younger generations. -Promote ministries through family settings where parents and children work together in things like community services, leading worship, prayers, and even after-meal cleanup.	-The Homecoming Movement is about the church living as a family again. -The Homecoming Movement brought together the first- and second-generation leaders as a family. -Church received prophecy from God to become an "International Family Center."
10. Needs in cross-cultural ministry	-Need for Sunday messages to be delivered in both English and Chinese, 50% of the time in each language with translation.	-Need for a very solid English children's program.

Figure 22 Common Themes of the two case studies

Summary

The two case studies, Ark Baptist Church and Forerunner Christian Church, show us an exciting and hope-filled picture for the future of local cross-cultural ministries of Chinese churches in the SFBA. We see there are many cross-cultural ministries already active in the Chinese churches. It is also the vision of the pastors of the two churches to reach the community and develop relationships with other local pastors of different ethnic groups and denominations. In the studies, we can see all seven aspects of missionary relationships, as listed by Wan and Hedinger. The two cases studies have ten common themes: church was started by Chinese pastor from overseas, church moved to a new location with a new vision, pastor joined local pastors network, desire for a bilingual environment to connect the first and second generation, cross-cultural ministry in community service, cross-cultural ministry in evangelism, cross-cultural ministry in church activities, passion to reach the local people in the community for Christ, an emphasis on the family, and needs in cross-cultural ministry. From Ark Baptist Church, we see an emphasis on building up the families. Through healthy families, the church can build up a strong bilingual environment where the first and second generations can work together in harmony to serve the community. From Forerunner Christian Church, we see the same emphasis on the family. The Homecoming Movement reunited the church family members to become a stronger and healthier spiritual family. The emphasis on building the relationship between the first-generation Chinese leaders and the second-generation English leaders strengthened the whole church family to serve the community. Through breaking down relational barriers, Forerunner Christian Church moves toward their global vision to become an "International Family Center." The "family" emphasis in the two case studies also aligns with the emphasis on the "family" in Chinese culture. Local cross-cultural ministries of Chinese churches should be promoted as an important and strategic ministry to fulfill Christ's Great Commission. Training in diaspora missions, relational paradigm, and cross-cultural ministry would be helpful in mobilizing Chinese churches to engage in local cross-cultural ministries.

CHAPTER 7
CONCLUSIONS

The Chinese churches in the SFBA have grown and matured to where they can engage in cross-cultural outreach to other diaspora groups or members of the host society. The Chinese churches have a rich heritage of diaspora missions from American Christians, and we should engage in diaspora missions to other ethnic groups in obedience to the Great Commission. "Missions beyond the diaspora" in the context of local cross-cultural ministry is imperative in light of the Great Commission and feasible without international travel overseas.

The authors believe there is a need to train Chinese Christians to think cross-culturally as they seek to fulfill the Great Commission. Chinese churches should not only undertake overseas missions to reach the Chinese, but also reach out to other ethnic groups, starting at home, because the Great Commission is to make disciples of all the nations or peoples. Chinese Christians in the SFBA work in companies and live in communities with a diverse population. More cross-cultural training will help Chinese Christians reach out to non-Chinese people around them as well as help them overcome xenophobia and ethnocentrism as they seek to serve Christ.

This archival research studied local cross-cultural ministries by Chinese churches in the SFBA. The authors hope this study will encourage Chinese churches to expand their local cross-cultural ministries in obedience to the Great Commission to serve and reach their neighbors for Christ.

The archival research describes how the Chinese came to the United States in large numbers starting from the 1850s. Despite periodic restrictions, they have become a sizable and successful community in the U.S. today. The Protestant work among the Chinese also began in California from the 1850s. Today, Chinese churches are growing due to Chinese immigrations over the years. In 2008, in the San Francisco Bay area alone, researchers counted 194 Chinese churches and attendance over 30,000.[621] There were 37 new Chinese churches started from 1996 to 2008.[622]

We see in the Chinese diaspora the hardworking nature, Chinese-oriented unity and fellowship, and harmony. The Chinese culture includes the avoidance

---

[621] Chuck and Tseng, 5.
[622] Chuck and Tseng, 4-5.

of confrontation, emphasis on relationship, high-context, and honor and shame. There is sub-cultural difference between mainland Chinese, Taiwan Chinese, Hong Kong Chinese, and other Southeast Asian Chinese. Among these ethnic groups are the OBC, ARC, and ABC, each having different levels of acculturation to the American society. Finally, the study presents strategies for Chinese churches to minister cross-culturally to other diaspora groups. The main overall strategies are 1) expand the international student ministries to include non-Chinese, 2) present the vision of diaspora ministries to the Chinese congregation, 3) and start new diaspora ministries in the community.

The diaspora mission strategies for SFBA Chinese churches are grouped according to the 11 cultural traits of Chinese and those specific to diaspora Chinese: 1) Industrious (hardworking nature), 2) Practice thrift and make sacrifices for their families, 3) Value education and social mobility, 4) China-oriented unity and fellowship among the overseas Chinese in friendship, partnership, and collaboration in careers, enterprises and investments, and social life, 5) Law-abiding and authority-fearing, 6) Confrontation avoidance (harmony), 7) Emphasis on relationship, 8) High-context culture, 9) Honor and shame, 10) Hybridization of lifestyle and cultural values, and 11) Bilingual and bi-cultural ARC and ABC. There are 10 ministry ideas listed for each cultural trait (total 110 ministry ideas).

The study discussed the historical development, historical perspective, theological background, and current issues in diaspora missiology. Diaspora missiology can be traced back to the 1970s in the Lausanne Conference and has been increasing and gaining more attention in missionary conferences. The Bible is also filled with the theme of migration. Christianity has been spreading via migration throughout its history. The brief history of different diasporas shows us the work of God in bringing the gospel to and through the diaspora. The relational paradigm and application to diaspora missions are discussed. The relational paradigm offers an effective missionary strategy in ministering to diaspora. Diaspora missions and relational paradigm are both ways to engage in missions to, by, and with diaspora people. We see that the value of relationships for Chinese people is woven into the culture. Thus, the relational paradigm is very applicable for Chinese Christian diaspora to engage in diaspora cross-cultural missions.

The study discussed relational paradigm, diaspora missiology, relational paradigm in diaspora missions, cross-cultural differences, dimensions of culture, Chinese culture, mentoring, cross-cultural leadership, and how to integrate them in local cross-cultural ministry training for Chinese diaspora to engage in diaspora missions. There were seven keys drawn from the topics of relational paradigm and diaspora mission. Seven keys were drawn from the topics of cultural differences, dimensions of culture, and Chinese culture. Finally, seven keys were drawn from mentoring and cross-cultural leadership.

Five implications were drawn from integrating relational paradigm with cross-cultural mentoring. From the implications, there is great potential to develop cross-cultural mentoring for Chinese diaspora Christians to engage in local cross-cultural ministries. However, more work needs to be undertaken to identify the right mentors and resources to do the training so that Chinese diaspora Christians can be empowered to do this mission work.

Website research yielded valuable information about the ministries conducted by Chinese churches in outreach and community service. While many of the ministries target Chinese people, there are many ministries that are cross-cultural or have the potential to be cross-cultural. The majority of the churches have English or bilingual services and websites. This is a good starting point to engage in cross-cultural ministry. The research shows that Chinese churches in the SFBA are well-positioned for cross-cultural ministry and already have been engaging in cross-cultural ministry. Since churches may not post every activity or ministry on their website, the website research shows only a partial picture of all the local ministries by Chinese churches in the SFBA. However, the potential of turning Chinese outreach ministries into cross-cultural outreach ministries is great, such as sports ministry, art, music, and education ministries.

Co-author Lei found most of the cross-cultural ministry activities from the English ministry websites of the Chinese churches. This shows that most of the cross-cultural community service activities are done by the English congregation members of the Chinese churches. American born Chinese may feel more comfortable and interested in community service activities than their Chinese parents because of their fluency in English and growing up in a multi-cultural environment. Chinese churches can recognize this and encourage their English congregation members in their involvement with community service and outreach. However, the purpose of this study is to encourage the Chinese diaspora Christians to be more engaged in cross-cultural ministries, not merely for the second generation American-born Chinese to be engaged in community service and outreach. Thus, the vision of local cross-cultural ministries needs to be shared to both the Chinese and English congregations of Chinese churches in the SFBA.

This study was based on the Chinese churches listed in *The 2008 Report: The Bay Area Chinese Churches Research Project Phase II* by James Chuck and Timothy Tseng. There are new Chinese churches which started since 2008. Future research should include new SFBA Chinese churches started since 2008.

For the purpose of equipping diaspora Chinese Christians for cross-cultural ministry, this study covers the background for cross-cultural ministries, diaspora missiology, cultural differences, Chinese culture from others' perspective, building relationships cross-culturally, communicating Christ cross-culturally, and practical suggestions to implement cross-cultural ministries in the overseas Chinese church in the SFBA. By having a vision for diaspora missions, we can move the Chinese churches from ethnocentrism to truly embrace a global vision of sharing Christ with all peoples. Local cross-cultural ministry training is an important part of equipping diaspora Christians to engage in diaspora missions beyond the diaspora. Through local cross-cultural ministry training, more diaspora Chinese Christians can catch the vision and passion to reach their neighbors who are not from their own culture.

Are all Chinese diaspora Christians called to engage in cross-cultural ministries? Certainly, as we are all called to be a witness for the gospel to our neighbors. Since the neighbors for the Chinese diaspora Christians in the SFBA come from different countries, it is natural for them to be a witness to their cross-cultural neighbors. This can be at work, at school, and in public settings. Many Chinese diaspora Christians in the SFBA may be doing cross-cultural diaspora ministries without knowing the term. Their heart for sharing the gospel cross-culturally may be similar to the scattered Jews in Acts 11:20 who shared the gospel not only with their fellow Jews but also with the Greeks. These Chinese Christians may share the gospel to their non-Chinese friends and invite them to church activities. Therefore, Chinese diaspora Christians in the SFBA have many opportunities to witness cross-culturally to their neighbors in their daily lives.

What about the calling to specifically engage in cross-cultural ministries? Co-author Lei have met Chinese diaspora Christians who are involved in an international student fellowship at a local community college. The students in the fellowship come from all different countries and most of them are non-Christians. Those who are involved as volunteers and staff are truly called to engage in diaspora missions cross-culturally. Also, Lei has seen Chinese diaspora Christians engaging in cross-cultural ministry in the park to teach English to Chinese and another ethnic group. These are examples of Chinese diaspora Christians being intentionally involved in cross-cultural ministries.

Through the internet website research, co-author Lei sees that many SFBA Chinese churches are doing local cross-cultural ministries, through community service. However, currently, Lei did not see many churches that are intentionally engaging in local cross-cultural diaspora ministries. Lei believes that this study shows Chinese churches in the SFBA have the resources and ability to do cross-cultural diaspora mission if they so choose. Therefore, the vision for diaspora mission needs to be shared with Chinese churches in the SFBA so that they can be more intentional in finding ways to serve and reach out cross-culturally to the diasporas who are not Chinese.

More studies can be done to survey churches about their local cross-cultural ministries. This can be part of the mobilization process as well. As churches are made more aware of their potential and calling to engage in local cross-cultural ministries, they may plan for more such activities. Currently, co-author Lei knows one Chinese Christian worker who is trying to start a multi-ethnic outreach ministry in the SFBA. The ministry currently includes seminars about different cultures and how to share the gospel cross-culturally, and teaching English in the park to Chinese and another ethnic group. Lei also volunteers with others, including some Chinese diaspora Christians, at a local international student fellowship that meets at an American church. Such multi-ethnic outreach ministries can be shared with the churches to form a network of churches that are interested in becoming more involved in diaspora missions. These churches can send their members to serve in local cross-cultural ministries. For example, the local international student fellowship mentioned by Lei is currently led by a member from a Chinese church. There are also Chinese mission conferences hosted by Chinese Christian organizations such as the Chinese Mission Convention (CMC) hosted by Ambassadors for Christ, Inc. (AFC). The theme of diaspora missions can be shared at these conferences to help mobilize Chinese churches to engage in more local cross-cultural ministries.

APPENDIX RECOMMENDED REFERENCES FOR FUTURE STUDY

Adeney, Miriam. *Kingdom Without Borders: The Untold Story of Global Christianity*. Downers Grove, IL: InterVarsity Press, 2009.

Conn, Harvie M. *Eternal Word and Changing Worlds*. Grand Rapids, MI: Academic Books, Zondervan Publishing House, 1984.

Crouch, Andy. "The Return of Shame." *Christianity Today* 59:2 (2015).

Davin, D. *Internal Migration in Contemporary China*. Basingstoke: Macmillan, 1999.

Djao, Wei. *Being Chinese: Voices from the Diaspora*. Tucson: The University of Arizona Press, 2003.

Douglas, J. D., ed. "Theological Education and Evangelism." in *Let the Earth Hear His Voice*. Minneapolis: Worldwide, 1975.

Dyrness, William A. *How Does America Hear The Gospel?* Grand Rapids, MI: William B. Eerdmans Publishing Company, 1988.

_____. *Invitation to Cross-Cultural Theology*. Grand Rapids, MI: Zondervan Publishers, 1992.

Escobar, Samuel. *The New Global Mission: The Gospel from Everywhere to Everywhere*. Downers Grove, IL: InterVarsity Press, 2003.

Fang, Serene. "A Brief History of Christianity in China PBS." <www.pbs.org/frontlineworld/stories/china_705/history/china.html> (June 2, 2013).

Fei, Michelle. "China Tops the List of Overseas Students in US." *China Daily*, November 16, 2011. < http://usa.chinadaily.com.cn/china/2011-11/16/content_14101404.htm> (June 2, 2013).

Fleming, Bruce C. E. *Contextualization of Theology: An Evangelical Assessment*. Pasadena: William Carey Library, 2005.

Fleming, Dean. *Contextualization in the New Testament: Patterns for Theology and Mission*. Downers Grove, IL: IVP, 2005.

Fuino, Gary, Timothy R. Sisk, Tereso C. Casino, eds. *Reaching the City: Reflections on Urban Mission for the Twenty-first Century*. Pasadena, CA: William Carey Library, 2012.

Fuller, W. Harold. *Mission-Church Dynamics*. Pasadena, CA: William Carey Library, 1980.

Griffith, Wendy. "Chinese Immigrants Find Faith in America." *CBN News*, December 26, 2011.
           <http://www.cbn.com/cbnnews/us/2011/June/Chinese-Immigrants-Finding-Christ-on-American-Shores/> (February 17, 2013).

Haines, J. Harry. *Chinese of the Diaspora*. London: Edinburgh House Press, 1965.

Heideman, Eugene S. "Syncretism, Contextualization, Orthodoxy, and Heresy." *Missiology: An International Review* XXV:1 (January 1997).

Hesse, Barnor. *UN/Settled Multiculturalisms: Diasporas, Entanglement, Transruptions*. London: Zed Books. 2001.

Hesselgrave, David J. *Planting Churches Cross-Culturally*. Grand Rapids, MI: Baker Book House, 1980.

_____. *Scripture and Strategy, The Use of the Bible in Postmodern Church and Mission*. Evangelical Missiological Society Series Number 1. Pasadena: William Carey Library, 1994.

Hesselgrave, David J. and Edward Rommen. *Contextualization: Meanings, Methods, and Models*. Grand Rapids, MI: Baker Book House, 1990.

Hexham, Irving, Stephen Rost, and John W. Morehead II, eds. *Encountering New Religious Movements: A Holistic Evangelical Approach*. Grand Rapids: Kregel, 2004.

Honig, E. *Creating Chinese Ethnicity: Subei People in Shanghai, 1850-1980*. New Haven: Yale University Press, 1992.

Hopler, Thom and Marcia Hopler. *Reaching the World Next Door: How to Spread the Gospel in the Midst of Many Cultures*. Downers Grove, IL: InterVarsity Press, 1993.

Hughes, Nora L. "Changing Faces: Adaptation of Highly Skilled Chinese Workers to a High-Tech Multinational Corporation." *The Journal of Applied Behavioral Science* 45:2 (June 2009), 212-238.

Hung, Vanessa, ed. *Chinese Missions - Towards the 21st Century*. Hong Kong: Hong Kong Association of Christian Missions, 1996.

Hunter, Alan and Kim-Kwong Chan. *Protestantism in Contemporary China*. New York: Press Syndicate, 1993.

Hwang, K. K. "Chinese Corporate Culture and Productivity." *Sun Yat-Sen Management Review* 7 (1999).

"If contextualization is good syncretism, is syncretism just bad contextualization?" <http://roxborogh.com/syncretism.htm> (10/14/2017).

Inch, Morris A. *Doing Theology Across Cultures*. Grand Rapids, MI: Baker Book House, 1982.

_____. *Making the Good News Relevant: Keeping the Gospel Distinctive in Any Culture*. Nashville: Thomas Nelson Publishers, 1986.

Jenkins, Philip. *The Next Christendom: The Coming of Global Christianity*. Oxford: Oxford University Press, 2002.

Johnstone, Patrick. *The Church Is Bigger Than You Think: The Unfinished Work of World Evangelism*. Pasadena, CA: William Carey Library Publishers, 1998.

Kam, I. and H. Bo. "Working with Sea Turtles." *ChinaSource*, December 19, 2011, 13:4. (Winter 2011). <http://www.chsource.org/> (6/2/2013).

Kohls, Robert L. and John M. Knoght. *Developing Intercultural Awareness: A Cross-Cultural Training Handbook*. 2nd ed. Yarmouth, ME: Intercultural Press, Inc., 1994.

Konieczny, Richard J. and Enoch Wan. "An Old Testament Theology of Multiculturalism." *Global Missiology* 2:1 (October 2004). www.globalmissiology.net <http://www.globalmissiology.net/docs_html/featured/konieczny_wan_ot_theology_of_multiculturalism.htm>

Kuah-Pearce, Khun Eng, and Andrew P. Davidson, eds. *At Home in the Chinese Diaspora: Memories, Identities, and Belongings*. Basingstoke: Palgrave MacMillan, 2008.

Kuan-Pearce, Kun Eng and Evelyn Hu-Dehart. *Voluntary Organizations in the Chinese Diaspora*. Hong Kong: Hong Kong University Press, 2006.

Kwok, Charles K. *The Chinese Churches in the USA*. Dissertation, Hartford Seminary, 2000.

Lam, Cyrus. *Serving With Your Gifts*. Petaluma, CA: CCM Publishers, 1994.

_____. *The Chinese Church - A Bridge to World Evangelization*. Pasadena, CA: Fuller Theological Seminary, 1983.

Lambert, Tony. *China's Christian Millions: The Costly Revival*. London: Monarch Books, 1999.

Larkin, William J. *Culture and Biblical Hermeneutics*. Grand Rapids, MI: Baker Book House, 1989.

Law, Gail. *Passing the Torch*. Pasadena, CA: Great Commission Center, 1994.

Leedy, Paul and Jeanne Ellis Ormrod. *Practical Research: Planning and Design*. 8th ed. Upper Saddle River, NJ: Pearson Prentice Hall, 2005.

Leong, S. *Migration and Ethnicity in Chinese History: Hakkas, Pengmin, and their Neighbors*. Stanford: Stanford University Press, 1997.

Lieberthal, Kenneth. "John L Thornton China Center Event," *Chinese Foreign-Educated Returnees: Shaping China's Future?* Held in Washington, D. C. April 6, 2010, edited by The Brookings Institution, 1-55. Alexandria: Anderson Court Reporting, 2010.

Lim, Christine Suchen. *Hua Song: Stories of the Chinese Diaspora*. San Francisco: Long River Press, 2005.

Lin, J. *Reconstructing Chinatown, Ethnic Enclave, Global Change*. Minneapolis: University of Minnesota Press, 1998.

Lingenfelter, Sherwood. *Transforming Culture, A Challenge for Christian Mission*. Grand Rapids, MI: Baker Book House, 1992.

Lundy, David. *Borderless Church: Shaping the Church for the 21st Century*. Waynesboro, GA: Authentic Media, 2005.

Luzbetak, Louis J. *The Church and Cultures*. Maryknoll, NY: Orbis, 1989.

Ma, Laurence J. C. and Carolyn Cartier. *The Chinese Diaspora: Space, Place, Mobility, and Identity*. Lanham: Rowman & Littlefield Publishers, Inc., 2003.

Marchetti, Gina. *From Tiananmen to Times Square: Transnational China and the Chinese Diaspora on Global Screens, 1989-1997*. Philadelphia: Temple University Press, 2006.

Martin, Mildred C. *Chinatown's Angry Angel: The Story of Donaldina Cameron*. Palo Alto: Pacific Books, 1977.

Murphy, R. ed. *How Migrant Labour is Changing Rural China.* Cambridge: Cambridge University Press, 2002.

_____. *Labour Migration and Social Development in Contemporary China*. London and New York: Routledge, 2008.

Myers, Bryant L. *The New Context of World Mission*. Monrovia, CA: ARC (division of World Vision International), 1996.

Naisbitt, John and Patricia Aburdene. *Megatrends 2000: The New Directions For the 1990's*. New York: Avon Books, 1990.

National Bureau of Statistics of China. "National Bureau of Statistics of China" 2009.

Nicholls, Bruce J. *Contextualization: A Theology of Gospel and Culture*. Downers Grove, IL: InterVarsity Press, 1979.

Nida, Eugene Albert. *Message and Mission.* 2nd ed. Pasadena, CA: William Carey Library, 1971.

Niebuhr, H. Richard. *Christ and Culture*. New York: Harper Torchbooks, Harper & Row Publishers, 1951.

Oberg, K. "Cultural Shock: Adjustment to New Cultural Environments." *Practical Anthropology* 7:4 (July 1960), 177-82.

Ong, A. and D. Nonimi, eds. *Ungrounded Empires: The Cultural Politics of Modern Chinese Transnationalism*. New York: Routledge, 1997.

Osgood, Cornelius. *The Chinese: A Study of a Hong Kong Community,* 1. The University of Arizona Press, 1975.

Osmer, Richard R. *Practical Theology: An Introduction*. Grand Rapids: Wm. B. Eerdmans Publishing Co., 2008.

Pan, Lynn, ed. *The Encyclopedia of the Chinese Overseas.* Cambridge: Harvard University Press, 1999.

_____. *Sons of the Yellow Emperor: A History of the Chinese Diaspora.* Boston: Little, Brown and Company, 1990.

Park, Chan-Sik and Noah Jung. *21C New Nomad Era and Migrant Mission.* Seoul: Christianity and Industrial Society Research Institute, 2010.

Parvin, Earl. *Missions USA.* Chicago: Moody Press, 1985.

Phillips, Tom, Bob Norsworthy, and W. Terry Whalin. *The World at Your door: Reaching International Students in Your Home, Church, and School.* Minneapolis, MN: Bethany House Publishers, 1997.

Pike, Kenneth. *Talk, Thought, and Thing: The Emic Road toward Conscious Knowledge.* Dallas: Summer Institute of Linguistics, 1993.

Poceski, Mario. *Introducing Chinese Religion.* New York: Routledge, 2009.

Pocock, Mike, Gailyn Van Rheenen, and Doug McConnell. *The Changing Face of World Missions: Engaging Contemporary Issues and Trends.* Grand Rapids: Baker, 2005.

Redding, G. and Y. Y. Wong. "The Psychology of Chinese Organizational Behavior." In M. H. Bond, ed. *The Psychology of The Chinese People.* Hong Kong: Oxford University Press, 1986.

Redding, S. G. *The Spirit of Chinese Capitalism.* New York: de Gruyter, 1990.

Ro, Bong Rin. *The Bible and Theology in Asian Contexts.* Taiwan: Asia Theological Association, 1984.

Roberts, Jr. Bob. *Transformation - How Glocal Churches Transform Lives and the World.* Grand Rapids: Zondervan, 2006.

Saunders, Stanley and Charles L. Campbell. *The Word on the Street: Performing the Scriptures in the Urban Context.* Grand Rapids: William B. Eerdmans, 2000.

Schineller, Peter. "Inculturation and Syncretism: What Is the Real Issue?" *International Bulletin of Missionary Research,* 16:2 (1992).

Seidman, Irving. *Interviewing as Qualitative Research: A Guide for Researchers in Education.* New York: Teachers College Press, 2006.

Shaw, Marty, Jr. and Enoch Wan. "The Future of Globalizing Missions: What the Literature Suggests." *Global Missiology,* April 2004. www.globalmissiology.net.

Shorter, Aylward. *Toward a Theology of Inculturation.* Maryknoll, NY: Orbis Books, 1995.

Sine, Tom. *Cease Fire: Searching for Sanity in America's Culture Wars.* Grand Rapids: Eerdmans, 1995.

_____. *Mustard Seed Versus McWorld: Reinventing Christian Life and Mission for a New Millennium.* East Sussex, England: Monarch Books, 2000.

Snodderly, Beth and A. Scott Moreau, eds. *Evangelical and Frontier Mission Perspectives on the Global Progress of the Gospel.* Oxford: Regnum, 2011.

147

Sowell, Thomas. *Migrations and Cultures: A World View*. New York: Basic Books, 1996.

Spencer, Aida Besancon and William David Spencer. *The Global God – Multicultural Evangelical Views of God*. Grand Rapids, MI: Baker Books, 1998.

Stott, John R. W. and Robert Coote. *Down to Earth: Studies in Christianity and Culture*. Grand Rapids, MI: Eerdmans Publishers, 1980.

Sun, W. *Leaving China: Media, Migration, and Transnational Imagination*. Lanham, MD: Rowman and Littlefield, 2002.

Tiplady, Richard, ed. *One World or Many? The Impact of Globalization on World Mission*. Pasadena, CA: William Carey Library Publishers, 2003.

Trompenaars, Fons and Charles Hampden-Turner. *Riding the Waves of Culture: Understanding Cultural Diversity in Global Business.* 2nd ed. New York: McGraw-Hill, 1998.

Tsu, Jing. *Sounds and Script in Chinese Diaspora*. Cambridge: Harvard University Press, 2010.

Van Rheenen, Gailyn. *Communicating Christ in Animistic Contexts*. Grand Rapids, MI: Baker Book House, 1991.

Wan, Enoch, ed. *Christian Witness in Pluralistic Contexts in the Twenty-First Century.* Evangelical Missiological Society Series Number 11. Pasadena: William Carey Library, 2004.

_____, ed. *Missions Within Reach: Intercultural Ministries in Canada*. Hong Kong: China Alliance Press, 1995.

_____. "Spiritual Warfare: Overcoming Demonization." *Global Missiology*, Oct. 2003. www.globalmissiology.net

_____. "Spiritual Warfare: What Chinese Christians Should Know and Do." 2004. Paper posted at <http://www.feca.org/bulletin_07/bulletin_07_warfare.cfm>

_____. "Spiritual Warfare: What Chinese Christians Should Know and Do." Published in *Global Missiology, Spiritual Dynamics*, Oct. 2003. www.globalmissiology.net

_____. "The Paradigm & Pressing Issues of Inter-Disciplinary Research Methodology." *Global Missiology*, January 2005. www.globalmissiology.net

Wan, Enoch and Michael Pocock, eds. *Missions from the Majority World: Progress, Challenges, and Case Studies*. Pasadena, CA: William Carey Library, 2009.

Wang, G. *China and the Chinese Overseas*. Singapore: Times Academic Press, Singapore, 1991.

Wardell, Margaret and Ram Gidoomal. *Chapatis For Tea, Reaching Your Hindu Neighbour: A Practical Guide*. Guildford, Surrey, England: Highland Books, 1994.

Willard, Dallas. *The Great Omission*. San Francisco, CA: Harper San Francisco, 2006.

White, Joey G. *A Historical Examination of Southern Baptist Church Planting in San Diego County, California School*. D Min dissertation, Mid-America Baptist Theological Seminary, 2009.

Wong, L. "Chinese Business Migration to Australia, Canada, and the United States: State Policy and the Global Immigration Marketplace." *Asia and Pacific Migration Journal* 12:3 (2003).

Wood, Gene. *Going Global: Networking Local Churches for Worldwide Impact*. St. Charles, IL: Church Smart, 2006.

Woodberry, J. Dudley. *Muslims and Christians On the Emmaus Road*. Monrovia, CA: MARC, 1989.

Yung, Hwa. *Mangoes or Bananas? The Quest for an Authentic Asian Christian Theology*. Oxford: Regnum Books, 1997.

Zhang, L. *Strangers in the City: Reconfigurations of Space, Power, and Social Networks Within China's Floating Population*. Stanford: Stanford University Press, 2001.

BIBLIOGRAPHY

Allen, Roland. *Missionary Methods, St. Paul's or Ours?* Grand Rapids, MI: Wm. B. Eerdmans Publishing Co., 1962.

Appleby, Jerry L. *Missions Have Come Home to America: The Church's Cross-Cultural Ministry to Ethnics*. Kansas City, MO: Beacon Hill Press of Kansas City, 1986.

Barker, Kenneth, gen. ed. *The NIV Study Bible*. Grand Rapids, MI: Zondervan Publishing House, 1995.

Bhandari, Sudhanshu. "Discrimination and Perseverance Amongst the Chinese in California in the Nineteenth and Early-Twentieth Centuries." *China Report* 47:1 (February 2011), 1-24.

Bosch, David J. *Transforming Mission: Paradigm Shifts in Theology of Mission*. Marynoll, NY: Orbis, 2012.

Chan, Sucheng. *Asian Americans: An Interpretive History*. Boston: Twayne Publishers, 1991.

Chang, Iris. *The Chinese in America: A Narrative History*. NY: Viking, 2003.

Chen, Lih-Chenh. *The Chinese Diaspora in Africa: A Pre-Evangelistic Ethnography of the Chinese Diaspora in 21st Century Africa*. D Miss dissertation, Western Seminary, Portland, Oregon, 2012.

Chuck, James and Timothy Tseng, eds. *The 2008 Report: The Bay Area Chinese Churches Research Project Phase II*. Castro Valley: ISAAC, 2009. <http://www.chinesecommunityumc.org/docs/File%20for%20the%202008%20REPORT.pdf> (February 17, 2013).

Corti, Louise. "Archival Research." <http://srmo.sagepub.com/view/the-sage-encyclopedia-of-social-science-research-methods/n20.xml> (4/18/2016).

Creswell, John W. *Qualitative Inquiry and Research Design Choosing Among Five Approaches*. 3rd ed. Thousand Oaks, CA: Sage Publications, Inc., 2013.

Denzin, Norman K. and Yvonna S. Lincoln, eds. *Handbook of Qualitative Research*. Thousand Oaks, CA: Sage Publications, 1995.

Denzin, N. K. and Y. S. Lincoln, eds. *Handbook of Qualitative Research*. 2nd ed. Thousand Oaks, CA: Sage, 2000.

Dyrness, William A. and Veli-Matti Kärkkäinen, eds. *Global Dictionary of Theology*. Downers Grove, IL: IVP Academic, 2008.

Edu-Bekoe, Yaw Attah and Enoch Wan. *Scattered Africans Keep Coming: A Case Study of Diaspora Missiology on Ghanaian Diaspora and Congregations in the USA*. Portland, OR: Institute of Diaspora Studies-USA, 2013.

Elashmawi, Farid and Philip R. Harris. *Multicultural Management 2000: Essential Cultural Insights for Global Business Success*. Houston, TX: Gulf Publishing Company, 1998.

Elmer, Duane. *Cross-cultural Conflict: Building Relationships for Effective Ministry*. Downers Grove, IL: InterVarsity Press, 1993.

Fernando, Ajith. *Sharing the Truth in Love: How to Relate to People of Other Faiths*. Grand Rapids, MI: Discovery House, 2001.

Fielding, Nigel, Raymond M. Lee, and Grant Blank. *The SAGE Handbook of Online Research Methods*. Los Angeles, CA: SAGE Publishing, 2008.

Friedman, Thomas. *The Lexus and the Olive Tree*. New York: Farrar, Straus, and Giroux, 1999.

Fung, Lawrence. *A Phenomenological Study of the Role of Pastoral Leadership in Mobilizing Chinese Churches in the San Francisco Bay Area for Global Mission in the 21st Century*. D Miss dissertation, Western Seminary, Portland, Oregon, 2011.

Genzuk, Michael. *A Synthesis of Ethnographic Research*. Center for Multilingual, Multicultural Research. University of Southern California, 2003.

Given, Lisa M. *The Sage Encyclopedia of Qualitative Research Methods*. Thousand Oaks, CA: SAGE Publications Inc., 2008.

Glasser, Arthur F. *Announcing the Kingdom: The Story of God's Mission in the Bible*. Grand Rapids, MI: Baker Academic, 2003.

Grunlan, Stephen A. and Marvin K. Mayers. *Cultural Anthropology: A Christian Perspective*. Grand Rapids, MI: Zondervan Publishing House, 1988.

Hegeman, Benjamin. "The Flight of the Swans: Discerning Hidden Values in Global Cultures." *Evangelical Missions Quarterly* 46:2 (April 2010).

Hesselgrave, David J. *Communicating Christ Cross-Culturally: An Introduction to Missionary Communication*. 2nd ed. Grand Rapids, MI: Zondervan, 1991.

Hewson, Claire, Peter Yule, Dianna Laurent, and Carl Vogel. *Internet Research Methods: A Practical Guide for the Social and Behavioural Sciences*. Sage Publications Ltd, 2003.

Hiebert, Paul G. *Missiological Implications of Epistemological Shifts: Affirming Truth in a Modern/Postmodern World*. Harrisburg, PA: Trinity Press Int., 1999.

_____. *Transforming Worldviews*. Grand Rapids, MI: Baker Academic, 2008.

Hofstede, Geert. *Culture's Consequences: Comparing Values, Behaviors, Institutions, and Organizations Across Nations*. 2nd ed. Thousand Oaks, CA: Sage Publications, Inc., 2001.

_____. *Cultures and Organizations: Software of the Mind*. London: McGraw-Hill Book Company Europe, 1991.

Hoke, Steve and Bill Taylors, eds. *Global Mission Handbook - A Guide For Cross-cultural Service*. Downers Grove, IL: IVP Books, 1999.

HonorShame. "About HonorShame.com." <http://honorshame.com/about> (2/28/2017).

HonorShame. "5 Keys for Relationships in HonorShame Contexts." <http://honorshame.com/5-keys-for-relationships-in-honorshame-contexts/> (2/28/2017).

Hooley, Tristram, John Marriott, and Jane Wellens. *What is Online Research? Using the Internet for Social Science Research*. New York, NY: Bloomsbury Academic, 2012.

Huang, I-shu. "Culture of the Chinese Diaspora." *China Report* 37:4 (November 2001).

Im, Chandler H. and Amos Yong. *Global Diasporas and Mission*. Oxford, UK: Regnum Edinburgh Centenary, 2014.

Khanna, Vinod C. "The Chinese Diaspora." *China Report* 37:4 (November 2001), 427-443.

Kim, S. Hun, and Wonsuk Ma. *Korean Diaspora and Christian Mission: (Regnum Studies in Mission)*. Eugene, OR: Wipf & Stock Pub, 2011.

Kraidy, Marwan M. *Hybridity, or the Cultural Logic of Globalization*. Philadelphia, PA: Temple University, 2005.

Kraft, Charles H. *Christianity in Culture: A Study in Dynamic Biblical Theologizing in Cross Cultural Perspective*. 25th Anniversary ed. Maryknoll, NY: Orbis, 2005.

Landis, Dan, Janet M. Bennett, and Milton J. Bennett, eds. *Handbook of Intercultural Training*. Thousand Oaks, CA: Sage Publications, 2004.

Lane, Patty. *A Beginner's Guide to Crossing Cultures: Making Friends in a Multicultural World*. Downers Grove, IL: IVP Books, 2002.

Lau, Lawson. *The World at Your Doorstep: A Handbook for International Student Ministry*. Downers Grove, IL: InterVarsity Press, 1984.

Lausanne Committee for World Evangelization. "The Willowbank Report." Lausanne Occasional Papers No. 2. Wheaton, IL. <http://www.lausanne.org/en/documents/lops/73-lop-2.html >

Ling, Samuel with Clarence Cheuk., *The "Chinese" Way of Doing Things: Perspectives on American-Born Chinese and the Chinese Church in North America*. Vancouver, Canada: Horizon Ministries Canada, 1999.

Lingenfelter, Sherwood G. and Marvin K. Mayers. *Ministering Cross-culturally: A Model for Effective Personal Relationships*. 3rd ed. Grand Rapids, MI: Baker Academic, 2016.

_____. *Ministering Cross-culturally: An Incarnational Model for Personal Relationships*. Grand Rapids, MI: Zondervan Publishers, 1986.

Looney, Jared. *Crossroads of the Nations: Diaspora, Globalization, and Evangelism (Urban Ministry in the 21st Century).* Vol. 1. Portland, OR: Urban Loft Publishers, 2015.

Moreau, A. Scott. *Contextualization in World Missions: Mapping and Assessing Evangelical Models.* Grand Rapids, MI: Kregel, 2012.

Muller, Roland. *Honor and Shame: Unlocking the Door.* Bloomington, IN: Xlibris Corp, 2000.

Nisbett, Richard E. *The Geography of Thought: How Asians and Westerners Think Differently...and Why.* New York: Simon & Schuster: Free Press, 2003.

O'Dochartaigh, Niall O. *The Internet Research Handbook: A Practical Guide for Students and Researchers in the Social Sciences.* First edition. London ; Thousand Oaks, Calif: SAGE Publications Ltd, 2001.

OM. "Religion." <https://www.omusa.org/areas/country/taiwan> (3/31/2017).

Ott, Craig and J. D. Payne, eds. *Missionary Methods: Research, Reflections, and Realities.* Pasadena, CA: William Carey Library, 2013.

Overseas Community Affairs Council. "Table 1: Overseas Chinese Population Count." <http://www.ocac.gov.tw/OCAC/File/Attach/1168/File_1860.pdf> (10/14/2017).

Paige, R. Michael, *Education for the Intercultural Experience.* Yarmouth, ME: Intercultural Press, Inc., 1993.

Payne, J. D. *Strangers Next Door: Immigration, Migration, and Mission.* Downers Grove, IL: IVP, 2012.

Piper, John. *Let the Nations Be Glad! The Supremacy of God in Missions.* Grand Rapids: Baker, 2003.

Plueddemann, James E. *Leading Across Cultures: Effective Ministry and Mission in the Global Church.* Downers Grove, IL: InterVarsity Press, 2009.

Pocock, Michael and Enoch Wan, eds. *Diaspora Missions: Reflections on Reaching the Scattered Peoples of the World.* Pasadena, CA: William Carey Library, 2015.

Rawson, Katie J. *Crossing Cultures with Jesus: Sharing Good News with Sensitivity and Grace.* Downers Grove, IL: InterVarsity, 2015.

Ritchie, Jane and Jane Lewis, eds. *Qualitative Research Practice: A Guide for Social Science Students and Researchers.* London: Sage Publications, 2003.

Roberts, Jr. Bob. *Glocalization: How Followers of Jesus Engage a Flat World.* Grand Rapids, MI: Zondervan, 2007.

Russell, Brenda, and John Purcell. *Online Research Essentials: Designing and Implementing Research Studies. 1* edition. San Francisco: Jossey-Bass, 2009.

SAGE Knowledge. Dictionary entry for "Archival Research." Class handout from Western Seminary DIS725. Spring 2015.

Stahler, Michael L. "William Speer: Champion of California's Chinese, 1852-1857." *Journal of Presbyterian History* 48 (Summer, 1970), 113-129.

Stanley, Paul D. and J. Robert Clinton. *Connecting: The Mentoring Relationships You Need to Succeed in Life.* Colorado Springs, CO: Navpress, 1992.

Ronald Takak. *A History of Asian Americans: Strangers from a Different Shore.* New York: Back Bay Books, 1998.

United States Census Bureau. "QuickFacts: Santa Clara County, California." <http://quickfacts.census.gov/qfd/states/06/06085.html> (4/8/2017).

Urga, Abeneazer Gezahegn. *A Reflection on Diaspora Cross-Cultural Evangelism: An African Perspective.* Kindle Edition, 2015.

Wan, Enoch. "(10) ARCHIVAL RESEARCH." Class handout from Western Seminary DIS725. Spring 2015.

_____. "A Critique of Charles Kraft's Use/Misuse of Communication and Social Sciences in Biblical Interpretation and Missiological Formulation." *Global Missiology*, October 2004. www.globalmissiology.net

_____. "Diaspora Missiology" *Occasional Bulletin of EMS* 20:2 (Spring, 7 2007), 3-7.

_____. *Diaspora Missiology: Theory, Methodology, and Practice.* Portland, OR: Institute of Diaspora Studies –US, 2011.

_____. *Diaspora Missiology: Theory, Methodology, and Practice.* 2nd ed. Portland, OR: Institute of Diaspora Studies, 2014.

_____. "Ethnic Receptivity and Intercultural Ministries." *Global Missiology*, October 2004. www.globalmissiology.net

_____. "Ethnocentrism." *Evangelical Dictionary of World Missions.* A. Scott Moreau, ed. Grand Rapids, MI: Baker Book, 2005:324-325.

_____. "Ethnohermeneutics: Its Necessity and Difficulty for All Christians of All Times." *Global Missiology*, January 2004. www.globalmissiology.net

_____. "Mission Among the Chinese Diaspora – A Case Study of Migration Mission." <http://www.enochwan.com/english/articles/pdf/Mission%20among%20the%20Chinese%20Diaspora.pdf > (February 17, 2013).

_____. "The Paradigm of Relational Realism." *Occasional Bulletin* 19:2 (Spring 2006).

_____. "Relational Theology and Relational Missiology," *Occasional Bulletin* 21:1 (Winter 2008), 1-7.

_____. "Rethinking Missiological Research Methodology: Exploring a New Direction." *Global Missiology*, October 2003. www.globalmissiology.net

_____. "Sino-Spirituality: A Case Study of Trinitarian Paradigm." *Global Missiology*, October 2003. www.globalmissiology.net

Wan, Enoch and Anthony Casey. *Church Planting Among Immigrants in US Urban Centers: The "Where," "Why," and "How" of Diaspora Missiology in Action.* Portland, OR: Institute of Diaspora Studies, 2014.

Wan, Enoch and Mark Hedinger. *Relational Missionary Training: Theology, Theory, and Practice.* Skyforest, CA: Urban Loft Publishers, 2017.

Wan, Enoch and Thanh Trung Le. *Mobilizing Vietnamese Diaspora for the Kingdom.* Portland, OR: Institute of Diaspora Studies, 2014.

Wan, Enoch and Tin V. Nguyen. "Towards a Theology of Relational Mission Training – An Application of the Relational Paradigm Enoch Wan and Tin V. Nguyen." *Global Missiology* English 2:11 (11-12, 2013).

Wang, Thomas and Sharon Chan. "Christian Witness to the Chinese People." *Perspectives on the World Christian Movement: A Reader,* 3rd ed. Pasadena, CA: William Carey Library, 1999.

Warner, Stephen R. and Judith G. Wittner. *Gatherings in Diaspora: Religious Communities and the New Immigration.* Philadelphia, PA: Temple University Press, 1998.

Wenzhong, Hu and Cornelius L. Grove. *Encountering the Chinese: A Guide for Americans.* Yarmouth, ME: Intercultural Press, Inc., 1999.

Whiteman, Darrell. "Culture, Values, and Worldviews: Anthropology for Mission Practice." Lecture given at the Overseas Ministries Study Center in New Haven, Connecticut, January 1999.

Winter, Ralph D. and Steven C. Hawthorne, eds. *Perspectives on the World Christian Movement: A Reader.* 3rd ed. Carlise, UK: Paternoster Press, 1999.

Wong, Bernard. *The Chinese in Silicon Valley: Globalization, Social Networks, and Ethnic Identity.* Lanham, MD: Rowan & Littlefield Publishers, Inc., 2006.

Woo, Wesley. *Protestant Work Among the Chinese in the San Francisco Bay Area, 1880-1920.* Ph.D. dissertation, Graduate Theological Seminary, Berkeley, 1983.

_____. "Presbyterian Mission: Christianizing and Civilizing the Chinese in Nineteenth Century California." *American Presbyterians* 68:3 (Fall 1990), 167-178.

Wurzel, Jaime S. and Nancy K. Fischman. *A Different Place: The Intercultural Classroom.* Newtonville, MA: Intercultural Resource Corporation, 1994.

Yang, Fenggang. *Chinese Christians in America: Conversion, Assimilation, and Adhesive Identities.* University Park: The Pennsylvania State University Press, 1999.

Yau, Cecilia, ed. *A Winning Combination: ABC/OBC: Understanding the Cultural Tensions in Chinese Churches.* Petaluma, CA: Chinese Christian Mission, 1986.

Yin, Robert K. *Case Study Research: Design and Methods.* 2nd ed. Thousand Oaks, CA: Sage Publications, 1994.